Genevieve S. McDaniel

MRS. SPRATT'S BUFFET COOKBOOK

Mrs. Spratt's
BUFFET COOKBOOK

Genevieve Spratt McDaniel

An Exposition-Banner Book

Exposition Press   Hicksville, New York

FIRST EDITION

© 1977 by Genevieve Spratt McDaniel

All rights reserved, including the right of reproduction in whole or in part, in any form or by any means, electronic or mechanical, including photocopying, recording, or by any information storage and retrieval system, without permission in writing from the Publisher. Inquiries should be addressed to Exposition Press, Inc., 900 South Oyster Bay Road, Hicksville, N.Y. 11801.

ISBN 0-682-48542-X

Printed in the United States of America

To
The Mrs. Spratt who let me cook,
(I was a full-fledged cook at nine).
The Mr. Spratt who ate my food,
Praised it, said it was fine.
The flock of patrons who came to eat,
Said kind words, and waited in line.

Jack Spratt could eat no fat,
His wife could eat no lean;
And so betwixt them both,
They licked the platter clean

Jack praised and talked about Mrs. Spratt's cooking so much that she bought lots more platters, invited in friends and neighbors, and promoted good cooking all through the neighborhood.

Mrs. Spratt could not cook and serve, too, so she set her platters and productions on the Buffet Table for all to come and help themselves.

Jack pleaded with Mrs. Spratt to write down the recipes of the different foods she cooked; to convert "a few pinches" into teaspoons and tablespoons, "handfuls" into cups; to list ingredients and amounts; to list the cooking time of foods; to name and organize her recipes.

This is how she progressed from Mrs. Spratt's Buffet Table to *Mrs. Spratt's Buffet Cookbook.*

Thus, these recipes for luncheon, dinner, or buffet have been compiled selected, and proven by one who has been in the restaurant and supper-club business for many years; by one who has supervised and participated in the preparation, cooking, and serving of hundreds of thousands of customer-approved meals.

GENEVIEVE SPRATT MCDANIEL
Oxford, Iowa

CONTENTS

HINTS   9

Part 1
THE HOT BUFFET

1. Beef   21
2. Ground Beef   33
3. Ham, Pork, and Other Meats   49
4. Chicken and Other Fowl   63
5. Fish and Seafood   81
6. Vegetables   101
7. Rice and Pasta   139

Part 2
THE COLD BUFFET

8. Hearty Salads   147
9. Fruit, Vegetable, and Molded Salads   155

Part 3
OTHER DELIGHTS FOR THE BUFFET TABLE

10. Appetizers   181
11. Soups and Chowders   185
12. Soufflés   191
13. Stuffing, Breads, and Dumplings   195
14. Sauces   201
15. Salad Dressings   211
16. Desserts   215

TITLE INDEX   223

HINTS

A watched pot never boils OVER.

※

Pineapple rings or tidbits may be placed in blender and blended on "CHOP," and used as crushed pineapple. Especially useful in gelatin, because the juice may be accurately measured this way.

※

To stretch whipped cream, place 1 egg white and 2 tablespoons sugar in blender; whip; then add whipped cream for half a minute longer.

※

Stuff a couple of paper towels in plastic bag with cleaned radishes or onions—keeps them fresh longer.

※

Clean green onions without cutting off roots. Store in plastic bag with paper towels. Cut off roots just before serving.

Carefully tear plastic wrap to line dish, pan, or ring mold for gelatin desserts or frozen salad. The contents can then be easily removed from mold.

Punch holes in bag of miniature marshmallows to let them dry out. They will soak up extra juices this way.

If your bananas will spoil before you can make banana bread, freeze the amount required for recipe. Take out to thaw a few minutes before mixing up the bread.

One of the greatest confidence games of all is cooking something from a recipe.

To prepare fresh chives. Pluck or cut chives off at ground level. Hold in hand and rinse under running water; cut crosswise with scissors.

Rub individual steaks or hamburger patties with cooking oil before freezing. They will keep and fry better.

Place eggs in refrigerator door space the same way as they are in the box—small end down for storage.

Hints

Save colored maraschino cherry juice or spiced apple juice for cooking rice or tapioca puddings to add color and flavor.

When making prepared cake mixes, place water and egg in bottom of bowl before adding mix. Mixes easier, quicker, and better.

Save and freeze small bits of leftover meat until you have enough to make a stew.

Save and freeze leftover sweet rolls. Soon you will have enough to make a delicious bread pudding.

If someone in the family is on a salt-free diet, try cooking a turnip with the boiled potatoes. It makes them taste as if salt has been added.

For the best tasting fried potatoes, place potatoes in pan when shortening is piping hot, turn heat down, and fry slowly. About 5 minutes before serving turn burner up, brown fast, and serve piping hot. This method makes much better potatoes than when browned fast and left to simmer and soak up grease before serving.

For 6 slices maple-cinnamon toast, mix 2 tablespoons maple syrup and ½ teaspoon cinnamon into ¼ cup soft butter or margarine. Spread on toast.

To store cleaned celery for several days; clean and place in refrigerator in jar of water.

When grating cabbage, rinse head and cut into quarters. Use slicing part of grater up to where the core begins, then turn grater to grating side for the rest. Hold quarters in flat of hand, so that knuckles are completely away from the grater. The texture of the cole slaw is better this way. Some of the core may be used.

To crisp lettuce: Barely slice bottom of core deep enough to remove discolored piece. Run water over head or dip it in cold water. Place it on sink drainboard *core down* for about 30 minutes. Wrap two sheets of paper toweling around the head of lettuce and place in a plastic bag. Store in crisper pan *core up*. Keeps several days longer than usual.

Beef or calf's liver does not need to be parboiled before cooking, but both pork and lamb liver should be scalded before cooking. Place liver in shallow dish, pour boiling water over it, let stand 5 minutes, then drain.

Hints

Add a piece of lemon peel to the cookie jar when placing fresh cookies in it. Keeps them fresh and crisp longer.

To make long, "curled" chocolate shavings, which give a professional look to your decorations for tops of cakes, pies, or puddings, use the vegetable peeler to shave the chocolate.

When stirring with a metal spoon, place the spoon over the handle of the pan if you must leave for a minute. Keeps your fingers from getting burned when you return.

To see if old yeast is still good, put it in warm water with a teaspoon of sugar and stir. If it begins to foam in 10 minutes, use it.

Never put salt in beans until they are almost done. It retards the cooking.

Doughnuts for breakfast: Use prepared biscuit tube. Punch hole in biscuit with thumb and forefinger. Fry in hot fat to desired shade, turn over, and brown other side. Drain. Roll in sugar or cinnamon or both.

To marinate liver: Place liver in rounded bowl. Pour equal portions of milk and soy sauce over liver. Marinate for half an hour. Drain. Dredge in seasoned flour. Fry as usual.

Pierce chicken livers with two-pronged fork to keep them from splattering when fried.

Many recipes call for running cold water over macaroni and spaghetti. This is to interrupt cooking, not because it needs to be rinsed.

Use powdered milk in cooking. When recipe calls for 1 cup milk, use 1 cup water, and stir in ⅓ cup powdered milk just before the end of cooking time. In a casserole dish, add water and powdered milk when mixing other ingredients.

Parboil potatoes before placing them in oven to bake. Place potatoes in kettle of hot water on stove and cook about 15 minutes. Remove carefully, so as to not break skins. The potatoes will bake in less time.

If you want to serve just plain corn for a group, buy a can of cream-style corn and a can of whole-kernel corn and mix together. Or blend half of 1 can whole kernel in blender and mix with the other half

Hints

Add a small pinch of soda to gravy that has grease floating on top. Watch carefully so that it doesn't fizz over. The soda homogenizes the grease.

ଊଊଊ

To fry or bake domestic or wild rabbit: Salt and pepper cut-up rabbit. Fry in cooking oil in hot skillet or bake in equal portions of catsup and cola beverage in preheated 325° oven until tender.

ଊଊଊ

To preserve color of red cabbage, add a tablespoon vinegar or lemon juice when cooking.

ଊଊଊ

If plastic bread wrapper gets burned to the outside of electric skillet, try cleaning with fingernail polish remover.

ଊଊଊ

To make a buffet table from a chest of drawers:
Measure length of chest; have a 9-inch wide board sawed to same length. Open drawers and cover with the board. Place cloth over top.

ଊଊଊ

When baking prepared biscuits in a tube, place two together, one on top of the other, to make bigger and better biscuits.

ଊଊଊ

White pepper is an indistinguishable complementary seasoning. The cook needs it for white vegetables and meats; use it for everything, for all foods' better appearance when served.

※

Cheat a little. Look at the frozen TV dinners in the supermarkets for a few new ideas as to what to serve as accompaniments to various entrees.

※

Clean the cranberries. Don't throw the bag of cranberries directly into the freezer. Clean them first. Wash, pick over, drain, and freeze. Replace in same bag (rinsed—there are recipes on it), tighten with tie twist and place in another plastic bag, because often cranberries come in punched plastic bags. When ready to cook, plop directly into hot water; or if grinding for a salad, grind frozen.

※

Keep a junk box in the freezer. Put parts of green pepper, onion, cut-up carrots, celery, and so on. Then when needed for stew or casseroles, either grate off some, or plop right into cooking water. Even leftover mashed potatoes may be added to potato soup.

※

Rinse canned Chinese vegetables, because they are slightly salty.

※

When slicing with a very sharp (or dull) butcher or slicing knife, put a pot holder between your hand and the knife handle.

Hints

You may at sometime lose a pot holder, but you won't ever have to go to the hospital to have your thumb sewed back on to the rest of your hand.

Cook a green pepper with the boiled cabbage. The neighbors won't know what you are having for dinner.

Don't throw away that sweet pickle juice. Buy a can of beets, drain, and add to the pickle juice for pickled beets. Or if you have a larger amount of sweet pickle juice, buy a head of cauliflower; clean, separate flowerets, and cook, watching carefully until just barely done. Drain and place in pickle juice.
Cooked carrots may also be added to the cauliflower.

To prevent a skin from forming on the top of refrigerated puddings, place transparent plastic wrap tightly over the top of dish. Don't let the wrap touch the pudding. Peel off just before serving.

If you like your pot roast "zippy," add a teaspoon or a tablespoon of horseradish to the braising liquid. If you like it with fruit, add dried fruit, mixed or plain, just after browning. Add extra liquid. Fruits will plump as they cook with the roast.

To shell Brazil or pecan nuts, cover with boiling water and allow to set an hour or more. Meats will come out in good shape.

Use muffin tins to bake your biscuits. Helps to make them crustier and higher.

That indented space at the front of your kitchen counter is toe space. Some of my employees thought it was a place to push the dirt.

Part 1
THE HOT BUFFET

1

BEEF

BEEF AND NOODLES

1 (2½-3 lb.) chuck roast
1 pkg. (12 oz.) noodles
2 cans (10¾ oz.) cream of mushroom soup
salt
water to measure

Cover beef with water, simmer about 1½ hours. Remove beef, measure broth; cut meat in bite-size pieces and return to pot.

Add noodles and enough water to make 8 cups. Bring to boil, forking noodles to separate; lower heat to simmer. Cook about 15 minutes. Add soup; simmer until done.

Makes 12 servings.

BEEF SOUPER

3 cups cooked beef, cubed
1 small green pepper, chopped
1 small onion, chopped
2 tbsp. cooking oil
1 can (1 lb.) red beans
1 can (10¾ oz.) tomato soup
1 can (10¾ oz.) cream of mushroom soup
1 can (11 oz.) cheddar cheese soup
1½ soup cans water
1 tsp. salt
¼ tsp. white pepper

In a heavy saucepan, sauté beef, onion, and pepper in cooking oil a few minutes. Add remaining ingredients. Simmer until heated.

Serve over mashed potatoes, hot biscuits, or toast.

Makes 8 servings.

Note: Use the same recipe for leftover pork.

BEEF STEW

2 lbs. beef, cubed into 1-inch squares
1 tbsp. cooking oil
water
2 onions, quartered
6 potatoes, peeled and quartered
4 carrots, peeled and cut in 1-inch pieces
2 cups tomatoes
1 turnip, peeled and diced
1 pkg. (10¾ oz.) frozen mixed vegetable
1 tbsp. flour
¼ cup water
1 tsp. salt
¼ tsp. pepper

Brown beef in cooking oil in a large heavy saucepan. Add 1 cup water. Cover; simmer for 30 minutes. Add onions, potatoes, carrots, and turnip. Cover with water; cook another 30 minutes. Add tomatoes and frozen vegetables; cover and cook another 30 minutes. Mix flour with ¼ cup water; add to stew. Simmer until ready to serve.

Makes 12 servings.

QUICK CORNED BEEF AND CABBAGE

1½ cups cooked corned beef, cut in cubes, or 1 can (12 oz.) corned beef, cut in cubes
4 cups water
6 small potatoes, peeled and halved
6 small white onions, peeled
1 head cabbage, cut in eighths, leaving core with piece
1½ tsp. salt
½ tsp. white pepper
2 tbsp. chopped parsley (optional)
prepared mustard

Beef

In covered saucepan, cook potatoes and onions in water about 15 minutes. Add cabbage; cook about 30 minutes. Add beef and seasonings; cook another 15 minutes. Serve with prepared mustard.

Makes 12 servings.

DRIED BEEF CASSEROLE

1 pkg. (4 oz.) dried beef, shredded
2 cups uncooked macaroni
1 small onion, diced
4 hard-cooked eggs, diced
1 cup milk
1 cup cheese, shredded
1 can (10¾ oz.) cream of mushroom soup
2 tbsp. butter or margarine
2 cups water (added to casserole just before baking)

Mix ingredients together in 2-quart casserole; let stand overnight. Bake in preheated 375° oven about 45 minutes.

Makes 4 servings.

FRIED HEART

1 small beef heart or ½ of large beef heart
2 qts. cold water plus 2 tsp. salt
3 tbsp. shortening or cooking oil
½ cup flour or fine dry bread crumbs
½ tsp. salt
¼ tsp. white pepper

Soak the heart in salted cold water for an hour. Cut either size heart in half and parboil for 30 minutes. Drain and slice in ¼-inch slices. Dredge with seasoned flour and bread crumbs and fry slowly in shortening until browned on both sides. Serve while hot.

Makes 4 servings.

HASH

(Beef, Pork, Turkey, or Chicken)

3 cups cooked meat, cubed
3 cups potatoes, cooked and cubed
1 can (6 oz.) evaporated milk, plus 1 can of water or (10¾ oz.) cream of celery soup
¼ cup parsley, finely snipped
1 onion, diced
2 tsp. Worcestershire sauce or bottled browning and seasoning sauce
½ tsp. salt
½ tsp. celery salt or seasoned salt
⅛ tsp. white pepper
2 cups beef or chicken stock or water
1 tbsp. butter or margarine

Combine ingredients; turn into pan or casserole. Bake in preheated oven at 350° for about 30 minutes (covered for 15 minutes, uncovered for last 15 minutes). Or combine ingredients in Dutch oven and cook the same way.

Makes 6-8 servings.

NEW ENGLAND BOILED DINNER

4-5 lb. corned beef brisket
6 small beets
6 small turnips, peeled and quartered
6 medium carrots, peeled and cut in 2-inch pieces
8 medium potatoes, peeled and halved
6 small onions, peeled
1 medium head cabbage, quartered

Place beef in large kettle; simmer about 3 hours. Add turnips, carrots, potatoes, and onions. Cook another 30 minutes.

Meanwhile, cook beets in separate saucepan. Slip skins from beets; add to pot.

Add cabbage to beef; cook another 15 minutes.

Remove beef and place in center of platter; slice; surround with vegetables. Serve a cruet of vinegar and jar of prepared mustard on the side.

Makes 12 servings.

BAKED CORNED BEEF HASH

1 can (12 oz.) corned beef, chopped
1 pack soda crackers (40 crackers)
½ cup water
1 cup onion, chopped
3 tbsp. butter or margarine
¼ tsp. white pepper
2 eggs, slightly beaten
1 can (lb.) whole kernel corn, drained
2 tomatoes, peeled and chopped
8 oz. cheese, cut in small cubes

Coarsely crumble crackers in large bowl; add water. Sauté onion in butter or margarine until tender, then add to cracker mixture along with corned beef. Mix in eggs and pepper. Pour into greased shallow baking pan (9-by-13 inches). Add in layers; corn, tomatoes, cheese. Bake in preheated 375° oven about 30 minutes.
Makes 4 servings.

BEEF STROGANOFF

2 lbs. round steak, cut in 1-inch pieces
¼ cup cooking oil
2 cups mushrooms
1 small onion, chopped
1 bay leaf
1 tsp. salt
½ tsp. white pepper
1 can (6 oz.) tomato paste
3 tbsp. flour
1 bouillon cube dissolved in 1 cup boiling water
¼ tsp. garlic powder
1 tsp. Worcestershire sauce
1 cup sour cream

Brown steak in oil in heavy skillet. Add onions and mushrooms; sauté about 5 minutes. Mix remaining ingredients, except sour cream; pour over steak. Cover; simmer about 45 minutes. Or place in casserole in preheated oven and bake at 350° for 45 minutes. Spread sour cream over mixture; cook or bake another 15 minutes.
Makes 6 servings.
Note: Serve over hot cooked noodles, if desired.

GREEN BEAN AND DRIED BEEF LUNCHEON DISH

1 can (1 lb.) cut green beans, drained
1 jar (4 oz.) dried beef, shredded
1 pkg. (1⅛ oz.) cheese sauce mix
1½ cups milk
¼ tsp. chili powder
½ tsp. Worcestershire sauce
1 tbsp. instant minced onion
1 green pepper, chopped

Mix sauce, milk, green beans, and seasonings in saucepan. Bring to boil, stirring constantly. Add beef. Simmer about 2 minutes.

Serve over hot biscuits or toast.

Makes 6 servings.

ORIENTAL STEW

2 lbs. beef stew meat
2 tbsp. cooking oil
1 can (10¾ oz.) cream of mushroom soup
1 small onion, thinly sliced
2 tbsp. soy sauce
1 tsp. salt
½ tsp. pepper
1 head cabbage cut in 1-inch pieces
1 can (5 oz.) bamboo shoots, drained
1¼ cups water

If the stew meat is not precut, cut it into ½-inch cubes.

Brown the meat in cooking oil in skillet. Add onion, soy sauce, water, and seasonings. Cook for ½ hour. Add cabbage and remaining ingredients; simmer for 1 hour.

Makes 6 servings.

PEPPER STEAK

2 lbs. round steak, cut in serving-size pieces
¼ cup flour
½ tsp. salt
¼ tsp. pepper
4 tbsp. cooking oil
1 pkg. (1¼ oz.) onion soup mix
½ cup water
½ cup catsup
1 green pepper, cut in strips

Beef

Combine flour and seasonings; dredge steak in flour and brown in cooking oil. Add soup mix, water, and catsup. Cover skillet; cook for 45 minutes. Add green pepper strips over top of steak; cover and cook until steak is tender, about 30 more minutes.

Makes 6 servings.

PIGS IN A BLANKET

2 lbs. round steak, cut thin and divided into serving-size pieces
4 strips bacon, cut in ½-inch pieces
1 small onion, chopped fine
½ tsp. salt
¼ tsp. white pepper
1 cup bread crumbs
½ cup hot water
1 cup flour

Brown bacon and onion in skillet. When done, remove, then brown round steak on one side. Remove. Turn off heat, but save drippings. Mix together bacon, onion, seasonings, and bread crumbs. Divide over browned side of steak. Roll edges of steak together and fasten with string, round toothpicks, or skewers. Return to skillet. Add hot water; simmer about 45 minutes, turning occasionally. Remove when done, then sift flour into juice in skillet. Add milk or water for gravy to serve over pieces of meat.

Makes 6 servings.

POT ROAST

5 lbs. beef (round, rump, or chuck)
1 cup flour
1 tsp. salt
dash pepper
1 onion, sliced
1 cup tomato juice
½ cup water

Rub the meat with mixture of flour, salt, and pepper. Place beef with small amount of fat in Dutch oven; brown on all sides.

Add tomato juice, onion, and water. Cover. Simmer for 3-4 hours.

Remove meat to platter or warming tray. Sift flour; add to juice for gravy. Add water or milk if thinner gravy is desired.

Makes 12 servings.

WINE POT ROAST

1 (3-4-5 lb.) roast (round, rump, or chuck)
¾ cup Chianti wine
2 tbsp. dark corn syrup
4 slices bacon, cut into 1-inch pieces
1 onion, sliced
2 bay leaves
4 whole cloves
½ tsp. ground ginger
1 tsp. salt
⅛ tsp. pepper
¼ cup cooking oil
1½ cup water
2 tbsp. cornstarch

Place beef in large bowl. In a separate bowl, mix the next 9 ingredients; pour over beef. Refrigerate overnight.

Remove meat, reserving marinade. Brown roast in cooking oil in Dutch oven. Remove bay leaves and cloves from marinade and add to beef, plus 1 cup of the water. Cover; simmer until meat is tender. Remove meat; mix cornstarch with remaining water; add to juices in pan; bring to boil; serve with roast.

Makes 8-12 servings.

SHEPHERD'S PIE

2 cups cooked beef or pork, chopped
3 cups mashed potatoes
1 pkg. (⅞ oz.) brown gravy mix prepared with 1 cup water
1 tbsp. diced onion
2 tbsp. butter or margarine
½ tsp. salt
¼ tsp. white pepper
¼ tsp. paprika

Combine meat, onions, and seasonings. Place half the mashed potatoes in bottom of greased casserole. Add meat; pour gravy over meat. Arrange remainder of mashed potatoes around edge of casserole. Dot with butter or margarine. Bake in preheated 400° oven about 30 minutes.

Makes 4 servings.

Beef

SPANISH STEAK

2 lbs. round steak, cut into ½-inch cubes
1 egg, well beaten
1 tbsp. Worcestershire sauce
1 tbsp. prepared mustard
1 small onion, minced, or 1 large green onion, sliced just up to the green
1 tsp. salt
½ tsp. white pepper
1 can (1 lb.) tomatoes, drained; reserve ½ cup liquid, or 4 fresh tomatoes, peeled and sliced, adding ½ cup milk or water
1 cup grated American or cheddar cheese
6 strips bacon, cut in half

Combine egg, sauce, mustard, salt, and pepper; add meat; place in greased casserole. Spread onions on top, then tomatoes, then cheese, and top with bacon strips. Bake in preheated 375° oven for 1 hour.
Makes 6 servings.

SWISS STEAK

3 lb. round steak, 1 inch thick, cut into serving-size pieces
2 cups flour
2 tsp. salt
cooking oil
1 onion, chopped
1 cup celery, chopped
2 cup tomatoes
½ cup water

Heat oil in a heavy skillet that has a cover. Rub steak with salted flour; brown on both sides. Add vegetables. Cover skillet. Cook about 20 minutes.

Turn steak, moving bottom pieces to top of pan. Cook about 15 more minutes. Test for doneness. About 5 minutes before serving, mix remainder of flour (sifted to remove any lumps) with water; add to pan for additional gravy.
Makes 6-8 servings.

TENDERLOIN OF BEEF STROGANOFF WITH WILD RICE

- 6 slices beef tenderloin, cut 1 inch thick
- ⅓ cup shortening
- 1 carrot, peeled and sliced very thin
- 2 stalks celery, sliced very thin
- 1 large green onion, sliced to where green begins
- 3 tbsp. flour
- 1 can (10½ oz.) beef broth
- 1 tbsp. catsup
- 2 cups sour cream
- 2 pkgs. (6 oz. each) white and wild rice with seasoning, cooked

Sauté beef slices in shortening until cooked to desired degree of doneness. Remove from skillet; set aside and keep warm.

Add carrot, celery, and onions to skillet and cook until tender; stir in flour and mix well. Add beef broth and catsup; cook over low heat until thick. Gradually add sour cream and stir well, then add beef tenderloin and cook until heated through, but do not boil. Place ½ cup hot rice on each plate; remove beef tenderloin from skillet and place on top of rice; pour sauce mixture over beef and rice.

Makes 6 servings.

TENDERLOIN TIPS IN BURGUNDY

- 2 lbs. beef tenderloin, cut into ¼ inch-by-2 or 3-inch strips
- 6 tbsp. butter or margarine
- 1 medium onion, chopped
- 1 green pepper, chopped
- 1 pkg. (⅞ oz.) brown beef gravy mix, mixed and stirred with 1 cup hot water
- 1 cup red Burgundy wine
- 2 tbsp. cornstarch
- 1 tsp. salt
- ½ tsp. white pepper

Using about one-third of the shortening to begin with, sauté quickly about one-fourth of the meat. Then add remainder of meat and shortening, as needed, to brown. Remove the meat

Beef

strips from pan as they are browned; keep warm. When all the meat is browned, sauté vegetables about 3 minutes. Combine cornstarch with wine; add to skillet with gravy mix and seasonings. Cook 2 minutes. Return beef to skillet; heat 2 more minutes. Serve.

Makes 6 servings.

TOMATO STEAK

- 3 lbs. round steak, cut into serving-size pieces
- 1 medium onion, sliced thin
- 1 can (6 oz.) tomato paste
- 2 cans water
- 1 bay leaf
- 1 tsp. prepared mustard
- ¼ tsp. rosemary
- 1 tsp. salt
- 1 tsp. white pepper

Brown meat in cooking oil; when meat is turned, place slice of onion on each piece. Blend tomato paste with water; add to meat; add remaining ingredients. Cover skillet; cook slowly about 1½ hours.

Makes 8 servings.

2

GROUND BEEF

CABBAGE ROLLS

12 large cabbage leaves
1 lb. ground beef
½ tsp. salt
½ tsp. white pepper
½ tsp. seasoned salt

1 cup rice, cooked
1 small onion, minced
2 cans (8 oz.) tomato sauce
¼ cup brown sugar
¼ cup lemon juice or vinegar

Cover leaves with boiling water for 5 minutes; drain on towels.

Combine meat, salt, pepper, rice, onion, and 1 can tomato sauce. Divide and spoon onto each cabbage leaf. Roll up, starting in heavy end of cabbage leaf. Fold end over. Place in heavy skillet, seam side down.

Mix together second can of tomato sauce, sugar, and lemon juice. Pour over rolls. Simmer slowly (covered) for about 1 hour. Baste about every 10 minutes.

Makes 12 rolls.

LEBANESE CABBAGE ROLLS

12 large cabbage leaves
1 lb. ground beef
1 lb. ground fresh pork or
  sausage
2 eggs
1 onion, chopped fine
½ tsp. salt
½ tsp. seasoned salt

1 can (10¾ oz.) tomato soup
½ cup catsup
¼ cup lemon juice
½ cup brown sugar
¼ tsp. ground cloves
½ cup white raisins
½ cup water

Cover leaves with boiling water for 5 minutes; drain on towels.

Combine meat, eggs, onion and salt. Mix with 1 cup of soup mixture. Divide and spoon onto cabbage leaves. Roll up, starting at heavy end of cabbage leaf. Fold end over. Place in heavy skillet, seam side down. Mix remaining soup mixture with other ingredients. Pour over cabbage rolls. Add water; simmer slowly for 1 hour 15 minutes. Baste about every 15 minutes.

Makes 12 rolls.

GROUND BEEF AND CABBAGE CASSEROLE

1 lb. ground beef
1 tbsp. cooking oil
1 cup onion, chopped
1 tsp. salt
dash pepper

3 tbsp. rice, uncooked
1 can (10¾ oz.) tomato soup
1 soup can water
1 small head cabbage, shredded

Cook ground beef in oil until lightly browned and crumbled. Mix in onion, salt, pepper, and rice; cook 2-3 minutes more. Add soup and water, and mix. Remove from heat.

Place cabbage in casserole; pour meat mixture over cabbage. Do not stir. Cover and bake in preheated 350° oven for about 1 hour.

Makes 6 servings.

CHEDDAR STEAK

2 lbs. ground beef
12 slices bacon
1 pkg. (8 oz.) grated cheddar cheese

1 can (3 oz.) sliced mushrooms, drained

Divide beef into 6 patties; place on saucer and flatten to ½ inch thick. Lay bacon over top of patty in circular shape. Turn

into skillet, bacon side down; fry until bacon is browned and crisp. Turn. Adjust heat to cook to your desired degree of doneness without burning. When almost done, divide cheese over top of bacon; sprinkle mushrooms over cheese; cook until cheese melts.
Makes 6 servings.

CHEESE BEEF LOAF

2 lbs. ground beef
1 can (11 oz.) cheddar cheese soup
¾ cup crackers, coarsely crushed
½ cup ripe olives, pitted and chopped

1 tbsp. onion, minced
1 tsp. salt
dash pepper

Combine ingredients. Place mixture in casserole dish. Bake in preheated 350° oven about 45 minutes.
Makes 6 servings.

EASY CHILI CON CARNE WITH BEANS

1 lb. ground beef
1 onion, chopped
½ tsp. salt
3 tsp. chili powder
1 tbsp. cooking oil

dash pepper
1 can (10¾ oz.) tomato soup
1 can (1 lb.) red beans, rinsed and drained
1 tsp. vinegar

Brown ground beef and onion in cooking oil. Add remaining ingredients. Bring to boil.
Cover and cook over low heat about 20 minutes, stirring occasionally. Serve over biscuits, toasted hamburger buns, or English muffins.
Makes 6 servings.

A BUNCHA CHILI FOR A BUNCHA PEOPLE
(Mild Chili Soup)

3 lbs. ground beef
3 onions, chopped very fine
1 can (1 qt. 14 oz.) mixed vegetable juice
1 can (1 qt. 14 oz.) tomato juice or 2 cans (1 lb. 12 oz.) tomatoes

1 can (6 oz.) tomato paste or ½ cup catsup
3 tbsp. chili powder
1 tbsp. salt
1 tsp. white pepper
2 cans (1 lb. 12 oz.) red beans

Brown hamburger in large heavy cooking pot; add onions; sauté until limp.

Add remaining ingredients. Simmer about 1 hour or until ready to serve.

Note: Drain and rinse beans with cold water; chili will keep longer. It will keep in refrigerator a week, or it may be frozen for later use. More chili powder may be added to suit your taste.

Makes 24 servings.

SALAD CON CARNE

1 lb. ground beef
1 onion, chopped
1 tbsp. beef flavor gravy base
6 drops bottled hot pepper sauce
¾ cup water
1 tsp. cornstarch
1 tbsp. cold water
1 head lettuce, torn in bite-size pieces

2 tomatoes, each cut in 6 wedges
1 onion, sliced and separated into rings
1 green pepper, cut in strips
½ cup pitted ripe olives, sliced
4 oz. cheddar cheese, shredded
1 pkg. (6 oz.) corn chips, coarsely crushed

In skillet, brown beef; add onion, gravy base, and hot pepper sauce. Stir in water; simmer 10 minutes, stirring frequently.

Ground Beef

Combine cornstarch and water; add to meat and cook, stirring until mixture thickens.

In a salad bowl, combine rest of ingredients except corn chips. Toss lightly, but mix well. Spoon on meat mixture. Top with corn chips.

Makes 6 servings.

GROUND BEEF AND DUMPLINGS

1½ lbs. ground beef
1 small onion, chopped
1 tsp. salt
3 tsp. chili powder
1 can (8 oz.) tomato sauce
1 can (1 lb.) tomatoes
1 can (1 lb.) whole kernel corn

DUMPLINGS
1½ cups pancake mix
½ cup crushed corn chips
1 egg
2 tbsp. cooking oil
½ cup water

In Dutch oven or electric skillet, brown beef and onion; stir in remaining ingredients. Simmer 10 minutes.

In a bowl, combine dumpling mix. Spoon as dumplings over meat; cover. Cook 15 minutes without removing lid.

Makes 8 servings.

EASY GOULASH

2 lb. ground beef
1 pkg. (8 oz.) noodles
6 cups hot water
2 cans (8 oz.) tomato sauce
1 envelope prepared onion soup mix

Brown beef in skillet or heavy saucepan. Add hot water and noodles. Bring to boil, forking noodles to separate; lower heat and cook about 10 minutes. Add tomato sauce and onion soup mix. Simmer about 10 more minutes.

Makes 8 servings.

HAMBURGER CASSEROLE FOR TWELVE

3 lb. ground beef
¼ cup cooking oil
2 green peppers, chopped
2 onions, chopped
1 cup celery, chopped
1 tbsp. salt
1 cup ripe olives, pitted and sliced

1 can (4 oz.) sliced mushrooms
1 can (10¾ oz.) tomato soup
1 cup hot water
4 cups spaghetti sauce
8 oz. mozzarella cheese
1 pkg. (12 oz.) noodles, cooked

Brown meat in cooking oil; add next four ingredients; sauté about 5 minutes. Add all other ingredients, except cheese and noodles.

Place noodles in large casserole or a serving pan. Pour meat mixture over noodles, mixing in so as to not disturb noodles on bottom of pan. Top with cheese. Bake in preheated 375° oven for about 15 minutes.

Makes 12 servings.

HAMBURGER SPAGHETTI

1 pkg. (8 oz.) elbow spaghetti, cooked
1 lb. ground beef
2 tbsp. cooking oil
¼ cup flour
⅔ cup dry milk
½ tsp. salt

1 pkg. (1¼ oz.) onion soup mix
2 cups water
1 can (10¾ oz.) cream of mushroom soup
1 cup bread crumbs
1 tbsp. butter or margarine

In skillet brown beef in cooking oil. Remove from heat. Add flour, milk, salt, soup mix, and soup. Gradually stir in water.

Return to heat, stirring constantly until thickened. Place spaghetti in casserole, pushing up sides to leave a well in the center. Pour meat mixture into center. Sprinkle crumbs and butter or margarine over top. Bake in preheated 375° oven for 15 minutes.

Makes 8 servings.

JACK'S CHINESE SPECIAL

1 lb. ground beef
1 onion, chopped
2 tbsp. cooking oil
1 can (1 lb.) mixed Chinese vegetables
1 can (10¾ oz.) cream of mushroom soup
1 can (3 oz.) sliced mushrooms
1 cup grated cheddar cheese
1 can (3 oz.) Chinese noodles

Brown ground beef and onion in cooking oil. Mix with all ingredients, reserving half the cheese and noodles. Pour into greased casserole. Top with remaining cheese and noodles. Bake in preheated 350° oven, covered for 20 minutes, uncovered for an additional 20 minutes.
Makes 6 servings.

EASY LASAGNE

8 lasagne noodles
1 lb. ground beef
1 onion, grated
2 cups spaghetti sauce
1½ cups cottage cheese
1½ cups mozzarella cheese

Cook noodles until almost done; drain.
Mix hamburger, onion, spaghetti sauce, and cheese. Place layer of 4 noodles in greased casserole. Cover with one-half of mixture. Repeat layers. Bake about 45 minutes in preheated oven at 350°.
Makes 8 servings.

MEATBALLS

1½ lbs. ground beef
½ cup cracker meal
½ cup milk
1 egg, beaten
¼ cup onion, minced
½ tsp. seasoned salt
dash pepper
2 cups spaghetti sauce

Combine all ingredients except spaghetti sauce. Form into balls. Place on cookie sheet.

Bake in preheated 350° oven for 30 minutes. Pour your favorite spaghetti sauce into electric skillet, bring to 225°; add meatballs and simmer for 10 minutes.

Makes 3-4 dozen meatballs.

PORCUPINE MEATBALLS

1½ lbs. ground beef
1 cup precooked rice
1 egg, slightly beaten
3 tsp. onion, grated

1 tsp. salt
dash pepper
2½ cups tomato juice
1 tsp. sugar

Combine rice (right from box) with beef, egg, onion, salt, pepper, and ½ cup of the tomato juice.

Mix lightly. Shape into balls. Place in skillet. Add sugar to remaining tomato juice; pour over meatballs in skillet. Bring mixture to a boil. Reduce heat; cover; simmer for 15 minutes.

Makes 16 meatballs.

MEAT LOAF I

3 lbs. ground beef
1 can (10¾ oz.) tomato soup
1 can (10¾ oz.) cream of celery soup
2 cups cracker meal, fine bread crumbs, or oatmeal

1 small minced onion
3 eggs, beaten
1 tsp. salt
1 tsp. pepper

To beaten eggs, add all other ingredients; mix well. Put mixture into 2 pans. Bake in preheated 350° oven for about 1 hour.

Makes 16 servings.

Note: Bacon, catsup, or barbecue sauce may be placed on top of loaf before baking.

MEAT LOAF II

1½ lbs. ground beef
¾ cup oatmeal, uncooked
¼ cup onion, chopped
1 tsp. salt

¼ tsp. pepper
1 cup tomato juice
1 egg, beaten

Combine all ingredients. Pack firmly into loaf pan. Bake in preheated 350° oven for 1 hour.
Makes 8 servings.

MEAT LOAF PATTIES

Use above recipe, reducing tomato juice to ½ cup. Shape into patties; flour lightly; broil or pan fry.
Makes 8 patties.

MACARONI GOULASH

1 pkg. (8 oz.) macaroni
2 lbs. ground beef
2 tbsp. cooking oil
1 onion, chopped fine
1 green pepper
2 cups tomatoes
1 can (8 oz.) tomato paste
1 can (4 oz.) mushroom stems and pieces
1 can (10¾ oz.) cream of celery soup

1 can (10¾ oz.) cream of mushroom soup
1 can (11 oz.) cheddar cheese soup (optional)
¼ tsp. chili powder
1 tbsp. sugar
½ tsp. salt
½ tsp. seasoned salt
¼ tsp. pepper
8 cups water or tomato juice

Brown hamburger in large heavy kettle, adding cooking oil. When meat loses its pink color, add onions and pepper; sauté for a few minutes until limp. Add all other ingredients; cook slowly for about 30 minutes.
Makes 12 servings.

PEPPER HAMBURGER STEAK

1 lb. ground beef
1 tsp. salt
⅛ tsp. pepper
1 tbsp. cooking oil

2 green peppers, cut in strips
⅛ tsp. garlic powder
1 tbsp. soy sauce

Mix beef with salt and pepper; brown on both sides in cooking oil. When almost done to taste, add peppers, garlic powder, and soy sauce to skillet; cook, watching carefully, another 3 minutes.
Makes 4 servings.

PLANTATION SUPPER

1 lb. ground beef
1 small onion, chopped
¾ cup milk
1 can (10¾ oz.) cream of mushroom soup
1 pkg. (3 oz.) cream cheese

1 can (1 lb.) whole kernel corn, drained
¼ cup pimento, chopped
1 tsp. salt
¼ tsp. white pepper
1 pkg. (8 oz.) noodles, cooked

Brown meat in pan; stir in remaining ingredients, except noodles. Turn noodles into greased casserole; add hot ingredients; place in preheated 350° oven for 15 minutes; or add noodles to pan and simmer 15 minutes.
Makes 6 servings.

RANCH-STYLE BAKED BEANS

1 lb. ground beef
½ cup chopped green pepper
1 small onion, chopped
2 cans (1 lb. each) pork and beans

1 pkg. (1⅛ oz.) barbecue sauce mix
½ cup water

Ground Beef

Brown meat; add green pepper and onion. Cook until tender. Stir in remaining ingredients. Simmer 15 minutes.

Makes 8 servings.

RIGATONI FOR TWENTY

1 pkg. (lb.) rigatoni (big macaroni)
1 lb. ground beef
1 lb. pork sausage
4 cups tomato juice
8 cups water
1 onion, diced
1 green pepper, chopped fine
2 cups stewed tomatoes
1 can (10¾ oz.) cream of mushroom soup
1 can (10¾ oz.) cream of celery soup
1 can (8 oz.) tomato paste
2 cans (3 oz. each) sliced mushrooms
2 cups spaghetti sauce
½ cup Parmesan cheese
1 tbsp. seasoned salt
1 tsp. salt
1 tsp. celery salt
½ tsp. pepper

Brown beef and sausage in skillet. Add onion and green pepper; cook until limp.

In a large kettle, place tomato juice, tomatoes, meat mixture, water, and rigatoni. Cook while stirring lightly, about 10 minutes.

Add remaining ingredients; simmer about 15 minutes.

Makes 20 servings.

SALISBURY STEAK

1½ lbs. ground beef
½ cup dry bread crumbs
1 egg, slightly beaten
1 small onion, chopped
1 small green pepper, chopped fine
⅓ cup tomato juice
cooking oil
1 can (3 oz.) sliced mushrooms
1 can (10¾ oz.) mushroom soup

Mix first 6 ingredients, plus ¼ cup of the soup. Shape into 6 patties.

Brown patties on one side in small amount of cooking oil. Place patties, browned side up, in baking pan; salt if desired.

Divide mushrooms and mushroom soup over top of each patty. Bake in preheated 350° oven about 15 minutes.

Makes 6 servings.

SPAGHETTI MEAT SAUCE

1 lb. ground beef browned, set aside or refrigerated
1 pkg. (8 oz.) spaghetti
¼ cup cooking oil
1 onion chopped
1 can (6 oz.) tomato paste plus 2 cans water
2 cups tomato juice
1 tbsp. sugar
1 tsp. salt
1 tsp. seasoned salt
⅛ tsp. garlic powder
1 tbsp. Worcestershire sauce
⅛ tsp. oregano
⅛ tsp. basil
dash white pepper
1 green pepper (optional)
1 can (3 oz.) sliced mushrooms (optional)

Place cooking oil in a heavy saucepan and sauté onion and green pepper a few minutes. Add remaining ingredients. Simmer, covered, for 1 hour.

Spaghetti may be cooked in this sauce, adding previously cooked ground beef, or all may be cooked separately and placed on plate with beef and sauce poured over cooked spaghetti.

Makes 8 servings.

SPANISH RICE

1 lb. ground beef
1 onion, chopped
1 green pepper, chopped
1½ cups tomatoes
1 cup rice
1½ cups water or soup stock
1 can (10¾ oz.) tomato soup or 1 can (6 oz.) tomato sauce plus 1 can water
¼ tsp. salt
dash white pepper
4 tbsp. margarine or butter

Brown ground beef, onion, and green pepper in margarine. Add remaining ingredients. Bake in preheated 350° oven about 45 minutes; or simmer on top of stove for 30 minutes.

Makes 6 servings.

STROGANOFF PIE

1½ lbs. ground beef
¼ cup onion, chopped
½ cup sour cream
1 can (10¾ oz.) cream of mushroom soup
¼ cup milk
¼ cup catsup
1 tsp. salt
1 can refrigerated biscuits (10 biscuits)
¼ cup Parmesan cheese

Brown ground beef and onion; drain off any excess fat. Combine with remaining ingredients, except biscuits and cheese. Pour into casserole; bake in preheated oven at 375° for 10 minutes. Place biscuits around edge of casserole; sprinkle with cheese; bake another 15-20 minutes.
Makes 5 servings.

STUFFED GREEN PEPPERS

6 large green peppers
1 lb. ground beef or sausage
1 small onion, grated
⅓ cup celery, finely chopped
¾ cup rice
1 can (6 oz.) tomato sauce
1 tsp. salt for beef; ½ tsp. for sausage
½ tsp. pepper

While preparing peppers, put rice in saucepan with 2 cups water; simmer 15 minutes. Drain, if necessary, before adding to mixture.

Cut a slice across the top of green pepper. Remove seeds and membrane. (Wrap tops, and place in freezer to use when grated green pepper is desired.)

Place ground beef or sausage in skillet; brown very lightly, and crumble. Drain; place in mixing bowl; add onion, celery, rice, 2 tablespoons of the tomato sauce, and seasonings. Fill peppers with mixture. Divide remaining tomato sauce over peppers. Bake in greased baking dish in preheated 350° oven about 45 minutes.
Makes 6 servings.

SUPER SUPPER

- 2 lbs. ground beef
- 1 onion, chopped
- 1 cup celery, chopped
- 2 tbsp. cooking oil
- 1 pkg. (8 oz.) noodles
- 7 cups hot water
- 1 can (10½ oz.) cream of mushroom soup
- 1 can (10½ oz.) cream of chicken soup
- 1 can (10½ oz.) cheddar cheese soup
- 1 can (3½ oz.) French-fried onion rings

Sauté beef, onion, celery in cooking oil in skillet or heavy saucepan until beef loses its pink color. Add water and noodles to pan, occasionally forking noodles to separate; cook about 15 minutes. Add the soups; cook until well blended. Pour into baking pan; top with onion rings. Bake in preheated 375° oven about 15 minutes.
Makes 12 servings.

SWEET-SOUR MEATBALLS WITH RED CABBAGE

- 1 lb. ground beef
- 1 tbsp. cooking oil
- 1 onion, minced
- ½ cup vinegar
- 1 tsp. caraway seed
- 3 whole cloves
- 1 bay leaf
- 1 egg
- ¼ cup bread crumbs
- ¼ cup chopped raisins
- ¼ tsp. nutmeg
- 1 tsp. salt
- ¼ tsp. pepper
- 1 small head red cabbage, chopped
- 2 tbsp. brown sugar
- 1 tart apple, peeled and diced

In a large heavy saucepan or Dutch oven, cook onion in cooking oil 5 minutes. Add next four ingredients; cover and simmer 5 minutes. Remove cloves and bay leaf. Mix ground beef with next 6 ingredients; shape into balls. Add to mixture in Dutch oven; cook until set and slightly browned. Remove meatballs. Layer cabbage, then apple, then brown sugar, then meatballs in pan. Cover. Cook about 30 minutes.

Ground Beef

Put meatballs on serving platter, surround with cabbage mixture.

Makes 16 meatballs.

QUICK TAMALE PIE

1 lb. ground beef
1 small onion, chopped fine
½ tsp. salt
2 tsp. chili powder
⅛ tsp. white pepper
1 can (1 lb.) whole kernel corn, drained
1 can (1 lb.) tomatoes
1 can (1 lb.) red beans, drained and rinsed

CORNMEAL TOPPING
¾ cup yellow cornmeal
1 tbsp. flour
1 tbsp. sugar
1 egg, slightly beaten
⅓ cup milk
1 tbsp. melted butter or margarine

Brown beef and onion together; stir in next 6 ingredients.

Mix cornmeal with last 5 ingredients.

Pour meat mixture into baking pan. Place small spoonfuls of topping over mixture. Bake in preheated oven at 400° for 25 minutes.

Makes 8 servings.

TAMALE PIE FOR A DOZEN

1 lb. ground beef
1 onion, chopped
1 green pepper, chopped
2 cans (8 oz. each) tomato sauce with mushrooms
½ tsp. garlic powder
1½ tsp. chili powder
¼ tsp. seasoned salt
¼ tsp. Tabasco (optional)
¼ tsp. pepper
1 can (1 lb. 14 oz.) small red beans, rinsed and drained

1 can (1 lb.) whole kernel corn, drained
½ cup cheddar cheese, shredded
1 cup ripe olives, pitted and sliced

CORNMEAL CRUST
2½ cups yellow cornmeal
1 tsp. salt
1 tsp. chili powder
5 cups hot water

In a large skillet, brown beef with onion and green pepper. Stir in other ingredients, except cheese and olives. Simmer 20 minutes.

For crust: Combine ingredients in a heavy saucepan. Cook, stirring constantly over medium heat until very thick (about 15 minutes). Spread evenly in bottom of slightly greased baking pan, about 9-by-12-by-2 inches.

Spread ground beef mixture over mush. Arrange cheese and ripe olives over top. Bake in preheated 350° oven about 30 minutes.

Makes 12 servings.

TAMALE PIE WITH NOODLES

2 lbs. ground beef
1 pkg. (12 oz.) wide noodles
8 cups water
1 onion, minced
1½ tsp. chili powder
½ tsp. Tabasco or ¼ cup hot sauce (optional)
2 cans (1 lb.) whole kernel corn
2 cans (8 oz.) tomato paste
1 can (1 lb. 14 oz.) small red beans, rinsed and drained (optional)
1 can (10¾ oz.) cream of mushroom soup
1 cup pitted ripe olives, sliced
8 slices American or cheddar cheese

Brown beef in skillet; add onion; remove from heat. Place water in large kettle; add noodles; cook until they boil; stir; turn down heat; add all remaining ingredients, except cheese and olives. Cook about 20 minutes, stirring and watching carefully.

Turn into greased baking pan; spread with cheese and olives. Bake 20 minutes in preheated 350° oven. Serve.

Makes 16 servings.

3

HAM, PORK, AND OTHER MEATS

GLAZED HAM

1 ham, canned, fresh, or packaged (8, 9, or 10 lbs.)
1 can (11 oz.) mandarin oranges or pineapple rings; reserve liquid
1 tbsp. cornstarch
½ cup orange marmalade
1 tbsp. aromatic bitters
1 tsp. dry mustard
1 tbsp. vinegar
½ tsp. ground cloves
whole cloves

Score top of ham in diamond pattern. Place on rack in shallow roasting pan in oven. Bake according to basic directions.

While ham is baking, drain juice from fruit; mix juice and all other ingredients except whole cloves in saucepan; cook over low heat, stirring constantly, until thickened. Set aside.

About 30 minutes before ham is done, brush with glaze, then about every 10 minutes thereafter, using up half the glaze. Remove ham from oven; decorate by sticking whole clove in each crossed line on ham; place orange sections or pineapple on ham, then spoon remaining glaze over ham and return it to oven for 5 minutes.

Remove from oven; place on serving platter. Sprigs of parsley may be tucked under outer edges of ham.

Makes 16-20 servings.

HAM LOAF

5 cups ground ham
2 cups cracker meal or bread crumbs
1 onion, grated or minced
1 tbsp. horseradish
1½ tsp. dry mustard or 2 tbsp. prepared mustard
1 can (10¾ oz.) cream of celery soup
2 eggs, beaten

Add ham and other ingredients to beaten eggs. Pack into greased baking pan. Bake in preheated oven at 375° about 45 minutes.

Makes 10 servings.

HAM-MACARONI CASSEROLE

2 cups cooked ham, diced
1 pkg. (8 oz.) macaroni
2 cans (8 oz.) tomato sauce
¼ cup butter or margarine, melted
1 onion, chopped
½ tsp. salt
¼ tsp. white pepper
1 can (11 oz.) cheddar cheese soup
7 cups hot water

Mix ingredients in saucepan; simmer for 10 minutes. Turn into greased casserole; bake in preheated oven at 350° for 30 minutes.

Makes 8 servings.

HAM WITH NOODLES AND MUSHROOMS

2 cups cooked ham or luncheon meat, cubed
1 can (3 oz.) sliced mushrooms, drained
4 oz. noodles, cooked
1 can (10¾ oz.) cream of chicken soup
2 tbsp. butter or margarine
⅔ cup milk
1 tbsp. sherry (optional)
½ tsp. salt
½ tsp. white pepper

Brown ham and mushrooms in shortening in skillet. And remaining ingredients. Heat and serve.

Makes 6 servings.

MOCK CHICKEN LEGS

1 lb. lean pork
1 lb. boneless veal
1½ tsp. salt
½ tsp. white pepper
1 egg, beaten
½ cup fine bread crumbs, cracker meal, cracker crumbs, or prepared breading mix
¼ cup shortening
½ cup meat stock or water
wooden skewers (as for apples) or tongue depressor sticks

Cut both kinds of meat into 1½-inch squares, ¼ inch thick. Thread meat on stick, alternating, until stick is one half full. Press together into drumstick shape. Add salt and pepper to breading. Dip sticks in egg, then roll in breading until it is used up. Brown slowly in shortening on all sides. Add the stock; reduce heat; simmer about an hour in covered skillet. Remove cover and turn occasionally.
Makes 8 servings.

BAKED PORK CHOPS

6 pork chops, cut ¾ inch thick
¼ cup brown sugar
6 slices lemon
½ cup catsup
1 tsp. salt
½ cup water
6 unpeeled potatoes, scrubbed clean

Brown pork chops in skillet.
Place chops in baking pan, arranging potatoes around outside edges. Sprinkle brown sugar and salt over the chops; place lemon slice on each chop. Mix catsup and water, and pour over top. Tear a piece of aluminum foil to fit over top of baking pan, and seal down corners. Bake in preheated 350° oven for about 1 hour. Uncover; bake another 30 minutes.
Makes 6 servings.

BAKED PORK CHOPS WITH APPLES

6 pork chops, cut ¾ inch thick
2 apples, cored and sliced in about ⅛-inch slices
2 small onions, sliced
6 tbsp. brown sugar

1 cup catsup
¼ cup Worcestershire sauce
3 tbsp. sweet cider vinegar
½ tsp. salt
½ tsp. white pepper

Place apples and onions in bottom of greased baking pan. Lay pork chops on top. Place 1 tablespoon of the brown sugar on top of each pork chop. Mix the liquids and seasonings; pour into pan, not directly over chops, so as to not disturb the brown sugar on the chop. Tear piece of aluminum foil to fit over pan, sealing down corners.

Bake in preheated 375° oven about 45 minutes. Uncover pan; turn chops; bake another 45 minutes.

Makes 6 servings.

BARBECUED PORK CHOPS

6 pork chops, cut ¾ inch thick
6 slices onion

1½ cups Barbecue Sauce (*see* Index)

Brown pork chops in skillet.

Place chops in baking pan with slice of onion over each chop. Pour ½ cup of the sauce over chops. Tear piece of aluminum foil to fit over top of baking pan; seal down corners. Bake in preheated 350° oven about 1 hour. Uncover; place remaining sauce over chops; bake another 30 minutes.

Makes 6 servings.

PORK CHOPS AND RICE

6 pork chops, cut ¾ inch thick
1 cup rice, uncooked
1 small onion, diced
⅔ cup chopped celery
1 can (10¾ oz.) cream of mushroom soup

2 bouillon cubes dissolved in 2½ cups boiling water
1 tsp. salt
½ tsp. white pepper

Brown pork chops in skillet. Remove chops and set aside.

Sauté onion and celery a few minutes in the skillet. Add rice and remaining ingredients. Cook about 5 minutes. Pour into baking pan and spread over bottom. Arrange chops on top. Tear piece of aluminum foil to fit over top of baking pan; seal down corners. Bake in preheated 350° oven about 1 hour. Uncover; bake another 30 minutes.

Makes 6 servings.

PORK CHOPS AND SWEET POTATOES

6 pork chops, cut ¾ inch thick
6 unpeeled sweet potatoes, scrubbed clean
6 slices unpeeled orange

1 tsp. salt
¼ tsp. white pepper
½ cup brown sugar

Brown pork chops in skillet. Place in baking pan with orange slice over each chop.

Make a mixture of salt, pepper, and brown sugar, and sprinkle over chops. Arrange potatoes around outside edges. Tear piece of aluminum foil to fit over top of baking pan; seal down corners. Bake in preheated 350° oven about 1 hour. Uncover; bake another 30 minutes.

Makes 6 servings.

STUFFED PORK CHOPS

Note: Have pork chops cut 1 inch thick; ask butcher to cut a slit in each one to make a pocket.

6 pork loin chops	STUFFING
6 slices lemon	1½ cup stale bread crumbs
6 slices onion	2 tbsp. melted butter or margarine
⅓ cup brown sugar	
⅓ cup catsup	2 tbsp. finely chopped parsley
¾ cup white dinner wine	2 tbsp. minced onion
¼ cup orange juice	1 apple, peeled and chopped fine
1 tbsp. wine vinegar or lemon juice	
	2 tbsp. white dinner wine, or vinegar, or lemon juice
1 tsp. salt	
½ tsp. pepper	

To prepare stuffing: Soften bread crumbs in melted butter; add parsley, onion, apple, and wine; mix well.

Stuff chops with stuffing, holding together with toothpicks or tiny skewers. Or thread string through large needle and tie, leaving 2- or 3-inch long piece for easy removal before serving.

Place chops in greased baking pan; top with lemon and onion slice. Divide sugar over each chop. Mix other ingredients, and pour over chops. Tear piece of aluminum foil to fit over baking pan, tucking in corners. Bake 45 minutes in preheated 350° oven; uncover, bake another 45 minutes.

Or brown in cooking oil in skillet on one side; turn chop; add onion, lemon, and other ingredients as for baking. Cover and simmer for about 1 hour 15 minutes. Remove toothpicks, skewers, or string before serving.

Makes 6 servings.

Ham, Pork, and Other Meats

PORK HOCKS OR HAM HOCKS

Use at least 4 pieces pork or ham hocks. Rinse and place in enough boiling water to cover.

Cover and boil 2 hours for pork hocks; 1½ hours for ham hocks.

Ways to serve:
1. Cook and serve as entree.
2. Add presoaked lima beans to hocks while cooking.
3. Cook and serve with precooked spinach or cabbage.
4. Remove from kettle, place in casserole with sauerkraut, and bake in preheated 350° oven last half hour of cooking time.
5. Put well-scrubbed potatoes in pot the last half hour.

Note: Do not add salt to ham hocks. If cooking pork hocks with beans, do not salt until done. If using as an entree, add 1 teaspoon salt and ¼ teaspoon white pepper to each quart of water used.

PORK STEAK

1 pork steak for each person

Method 1: Dip in seasoned flour and fry on both sides in shortening until well done. Make gravy for mashed potatoes with the drippings.

Method 2: Dip in beaten egg, then in seasoned flour or breading and fry as above.

Method 3: Fry in seasoned flour and serve over precooked rice.

Method 4: Brown quickly in skillet; pour liberal amount of Barbecue Sauce (*see* Index) over steaks, and simmer 30 minutes.

BARBECUED RIBS

Use:
- Beef short ribs—1 or 2 pieces for each person
- Country style pork ribs—1 or 2 pieces for each person
- Spare ribs (pork)—estimate number of pieces for each person

Cook ribs in roasting pan, covered, in preheated 350° oven for 30 minutes. Uncover; cook at least 20 more minutes. Spread Barbecue Sauce (*see* Index) liberally over each piece. Cook at least another 15 minutes.

SWEET 'N' SOUR PORK ORIENTAL

- 2 lbs. lean pork, cut into ½-inch cubes
- 1 egg beaten
- ½ cup flour
- 1¾ cup water
- ½ cup cooking oil
- ⅔ cup brown sugar
- ½ cup vinegar
- ½ cup molasses
- 1 can (1 lb.) tomatoes or 4 fresh tomatoes, peeled and quartered
- 2 green peppers, cut in strips
- 1 can (15¼ oz.) pineapple chunks, drained; reserve juice
- 2 tbsp. cornstarch
- 1 tbsp. soy sauce
- 1 tsp. salt
- ½ tsp. white pepper

Combine egg, flour, and 1 cup of the water to make a batter.

Dip pork pieces into batter and fry in hot oil for about 10 minutes. While pork is frying combine brown sugar, vinegar, and molasses. Remove pork from skillet; add this mixture and tomatoes to skillet. (If canned tomatoes are used, add tomatoes and juice. If fresh tomatoes are used add the remaining ¾ cup water.)

Combine cornstarch with pineapple juice; add it to skillet. Add green pepper, stirring until mixture thickens. Add pineapple chunks, soy sauce, and seasonings; stir; then return pork to skillet; simmer 10 minutes.

Makes 6 servings.

KNOCKWURST WITH SAUERKRAUT AND SWEET POTATOES

4 or 6 knockwurst
1½ lb. sweet potatoes, cut into 1-inch cubes
1 can (1 lb. 11 oz.) sauerkraut, drained
1 tsp. caraway seed
3 tbsp. butter or margarine
1 tart apple, peeled and sliced thin

If raw potatoes are used, scrub and cook in salted water about 20 minutes. Peel and cut in cubes.

Mix all ingredients in casserole, topping with knockwurst. Bake in preheated oven at 375° about 30 minutes.

Makes 4-6 servings.

LAMB CURRY

1½ lb. lamb, cut into 1-inch cubes
1 onion, sliced
1 cup celery, chopped
2 tbsp. cooking oil
¼ cup flour
2 tsp. curry powder
1 tsp. salt
¼ tsp. white pepper
1 can (1 lb.) condensed beef or chicken broth
½ cup mint flavored apple jelly
4 cups hot cooked rice

Brown meat, onion, and celery in cooking oil; add flour and seasonings; mix well. Stir in broth and jelly. Cover; simmer about 1½ hours. Serve over rice.

Makes 6 servings.

IRISH STEW

2½ lbs. shoulder of lamb, cut into 1-inch pieces
2 carrots, cut in 1-inch pieces
6 small onions, chopped
4 potatoes, cubed
1 tsp. salt
¼ tsp. white pepper
4 cups water
chopped parsley

Cook the meat in the water for about 30 minutes. Skim off any excess fat. Add remaining ingredients. Cook another 30 minutes. Serve.

Makes 8 servings.

LIVER LOAF

1½ lbs. liver, ground or cut into ¼-inch cubes
1½ cups bread crumbs
1 onion, minced
2 eggs, beaten

1 cup milk or 1 cup water and ⅓ cup dry powdered milk
1 tsp. salt
½ tsp. white pepper

Add bread crumbs to beaten egg. Mix in remaining ingredients. Place into greased loaf baking pan. Bake in preheated 350° oven 1 hour.

Makes 6 servings.

RABBIT LOAF

1 rabbit
1 green pepper, cut into quarters with seeds removed
4 potatoes, peeled and quartered
4 cups water
4 tbsp. butter or margarine or bacon drippings

1 tsp. salt
½ tsp. white pepper
½ cup stock
½ cup flour
2 eggs

Put rabbit, green pepper, and potatoes in water in a large saucepan; cover; boil 30 minutes. Remove from pan. Remove rabbit meat from bone. Run potatoes, green pepper, and rabbit meat through coarse blade of food chopper. Strain stock and measure ½ cup, then set aside rest of stock for gravy. Beat eggs; add measured stock, flour, and seasoning to rabbit mixture. Place in greased baking dish; bake 45 minutes in preheated 350° oven. Make gravy from remaining stock; serve with mashed potatoes.

Makes 4 servings.

CHOP SUEY

1 lb. cooked and cubed beef, pork, chicken, or shrimp
4 cups water or beef or chicken stock
2 cups diced celery
2 medium onions, sliced
¼ cup cornstarch mixed with ¼ cup water
2 tbsp. soy sauce
2 tbsp. molasses
1 tbsp. bottled browning and seasoning sauce
1 can (6 oz.) mushroom stems and pieces
1 can (10¾ oz.) cream of mushroom soup
1 can (10¾ oz.) cream of celery soup
2 cans (1 lb.) Chinese vegetables, drained and rinsed

Add stock or water to a large heavy cooking pot. Cook celery and onion about 5 minutes. Add remaining ingredients. Simmer about 30 minutes. Serve with hot cooked rice.

Makes 8 servings.

Note: For variety, add a 5-oz. can bamboo shoots, drained and rinsed, or a 5-oz. can water chestnuts, drained, rinsed and sliced; or use fancy Chinese vegetables. (Drain and rinse Chinese vegetables because they are usually packed in slightly salted water.)

For Chow Mein, serve with Chinese noodles.

SAUSAGE AND SUCCOTASH

1 lb. Polish sausage, cocktail sausages, or regular sausage

See Index for Succotash; omit butter or margarine. Mix with sausage; heat and serve.

Note:

1. If Polish sausage is used, peel, slice into ½-inch slices, and brown in small amount of butter or margarine.

2. If cocktail sausages are used, add them.

3. If regular sausage is used, form 1-inch patties and fry until browned, pouring off any excess fat.

SCRAPPLE

½ lb. pork sausage, cooked and drained or shredded pieces of cooked pork
1 cup cornmeal
1 tsp. salt
dash white pepper
1 cup cold water
3 cups boiling water
2 tsp. diced onions

In a saucepan bring water to a boil. Combine other ingredients in cold water and add to boiling water. Cook, stirring constantly, until very thick.

Pour mixture into a greased loaf pan. Refrigerate several hours or overnight. When cold, cut into ½-inch slices; dip in flour or corn meal; fry in very hot fat on both sides. Serve hot with syrup.

Makes 6 servings.

SPAM* POLYNESIAN

2 cans (12 oz. each) SPAM, sliced
2 tbsp. cooking oil
1 medium onion, sliced
1 green pepper, cut in 1-inch squares
1 can (13 oz.) pineapple chunks; reserve liquid
¼ cup brown sugar
1 cup chicken bouillon (2 cubes, dissolved in 1 cup water)
¼ cup vinegar
2 tbsp. cornstarch
2 tbsp. soy sauce
1 orange, peeled and sectioned, or ½ cup mandarin orange sections

Slice SPAM; brown in oil in skillet; remove from skillet. Add green pepper and onions; sauté about 5 minutes. Add pineapple liquid, bouillon, brown sugar, and vinegar. Mix together cornstarch and soy sauce; add to mixture and stir. Heat until sauce thickens and turns clear. Add pineapple and meat; simmer a few minutes. Serve.

Makes 8 servings.

---

*SPAM is a registered trademark.

VEAL PARMESAN

4 veal cutlets
1 egg beaten
½ cup bread crumbs
2 tbsp. shortening
1 can (10¾ oz.) cream of tomato soup
½ soup can of water
4 tbsp. minced onion
⅛ tsp. garlic powder
dash thyme
4 oz. mozzarella cheese
4 tsp. Parmesan cheese

Dip cutlets in egg, then in bread crumbs. Fry cutlets in shortening in skillet until browned. Add rest of ingredients, except the cheese. Cover and cook over low heat until meat is tender, about 30 minutes. Add the cheese; cook a few more minutes until cheese melts. Divide sauce over cutlets.
Makes 4 servings.

VENISON WITH ONIONS

6 venison steaks
3 onions, sliced
1 cup water
1 cup sour cream
½ tsp. salt
dash pepper
4 tbsp. butter or margarine
4 cups cooked wild rice or 6 baked potatoes

Brown steaks in butter or margarine. As steaks are browned, place in Dutch oven and layer with onions. When onions are browned, pour drippings over steaks; add water and salt and pepper. Cook about 1 hour in covered pan or until meat is fork tender. Remove meat; place on platter; add sour cream to pan and heat but do not boil; pour over steaks. Serve with wild rice or baked potatoes.
Makes 6 servings.

4

CHICKEN AND OTHER FOWL

CHICKEN-ASPARAGUS CASSEROLE

- 2 cups cooked chicken, diced
- 3½ cups water
- 1 pkg. (10 oz.) frozen chopped asparagus
- 2 tbsp. minced onion
- ½ cup chopped celery
- 2 tbsp. butter or margarine
- 1 can (10¾ oz.) cream of chicken soup
- ½ tsp. salt
- ¼ tsp. white pepper
- 1 tbsp. lemon juice
- 1½ cup rice
- 8 pitted ripe olives, sliced

Place asparagus, rice, butter or margarine, celery, and onion in saucepan with water. Bring to boil; turn down heat; simmer while preparing other ingredients, or about 10 minutes.

Mix remaining ingredients, then mix all together. Pour into greased casserole; bake in preheated oven at 350° about 30 minutes.

Makes 6 servings.

BARBECUED CHICKEN

- 1 fryer chicken, cut in quarters
- salt
- cooking oil
- Barbecue Sauce (*see* Index)

Prepare chicken; brush with oil, rub on salt, and place on grill. Grill about 20 minutes. Brush with Barbecue Sauce about every 10 minutes. Continue cooking until done.

Makes 4 servings.

CHICKEN BASQUE

3 cups cooked chicken, cubed
1 lb. hot Italian or Polish sausage rolls
1 cup water
2 green peppers, cut in strips
½ tsp. garlic powder

1 can (1 lb. 12 oz.) tomatoes
1 can (8 oz.) tomato sauce
2 tsp. paprika
1 tsp. oregano
½ tsp. salt
¼ tsp. white pepper

Prick skins of sausage and place in skillet with water; bring to boil; cook for 10 minutes. Drain water off, then slice sausage in ¼-inch slices; return to skillet to brown. Lay green peppers in skillet around edge, away from intense heat; push and turn peppers while sausage is browning.

Stir in remaining ingredients. Mix. Cover; cook for 15 minutes.

Makes 8 servings.

CHICKEN CACCIATORE

1 (2½-3 lb.) chicken, cut up
cooking oil
1 can (10¾ oz.) tomato soup
¼ cup water
¼ cup dry red wine or 1 tbsp. vinegar

¼ tsp. garlic powder (optional)
1 tsp. crushed oregano
¼ tsp. salt
1 small green pepper, cut in strips
1 small onion, sliced

Brown chicken quickly in skillet in cooking oil. Pour off fat. Add remaining ingredients. Cover; cook over low heat about 45 minutes.

Makes 4 servings.

CHICKEN CASSEROLE I

2 cups chicken, cooked and diced
2 cups diced celery
2 tbsp. diced onion
1 cup mayonnaise or salad dressing

2 tbsp. lemon juice
½ tsp. salt
½ cup shredded cheese
1 pkg. (1⅛ oz.) potato chips

Combine ingredients, except cheese and chips. Pour into greased casserole. Sprinkle with cheese and chips. Bake in preheated oven at 375° for 30 minutes.
Makes 4 servings.
Note: Leftover turkey or roast may be substituted for the chicken.

CHICKEN CASSEROLE II

2 cups chicken, cooked and diced
1 can (10¾ oz.) cream of mushroom or cream of chicken soup
1 can (10¾ oz.) cream of celery soup

1 small onion, chopped
¼ cup cashew nuts
½ cup water or chicken broth
1 can (3 oz.) Chinese noodles

Mix ingredients, saving one half of Chinese noodles for topping. Pour into greased casserole. Top with noodles. Bake in preheated 350° oven for 30 minutes.
Makes 4 servings.
Note: Leftover turkey or roast pork may be substituted for the chicken.

CHICKEN CROQUETTES

2 cups cooked chicken, shredded
2 tbsp. butter or margarine, melted
½ cup flour
1 cup milk
¼ tsp. salt
⅛ tsp. white pepper
1 tsp. chopped parsley
¼ tsp. celery salt
1 tsp. lemon juice
2 eggs, beaten
crumbs or breading mix
cooking oil

Mix flour with melted margarine or butter; stir in remaining ingredients, except eggs and breading. Shape into patties; dip patties in egg, then roll in breading. Fry in hot cooking oil until browned. Or fry in French fryer set at 350°.
Makes 12 croquettes.

DRAMBUIE CHICKEN

2 (2½-3 lb.) frying chickens, whole
1 cup Drambuie
1 lemon (juice and grated rind)
¼ lb. butter or margarine, melted
2 tbsp. soy sauce
1 tsp. salt
¼ tsp. white pepper

Combine ingredients for sauce in a saucepan; heat, then pour over chickens as they roast in preheated oven at 375°. Baste with sauce about every 15 minutes. Roasting time is about 2 hours.
Makes 6-8 servings.

EASY CHICKEN AND RICE CASSEROLE

2 boxes (6 oz. each) prepared white and wild rice mixed with seasonings
5 cups hot water
1 can (10¾ oz.) cream of chicken soup or 1 cup cooked chicken, diced

Cook rice in covered saucepan with hot water for 10 minutes. Remove from heat; stir in chicken or soup. Turn into greased casserole; bake in preheated 350° oven for 30 minutes.
Makes 6 servings.

FIESTA CHICKEN BAKE

1 (2½-3 lb.) chicken, cut up
¼ cup flour
1 tsp. salt
⅛ tsp. white pepper
  cooking oil
1 pkg. (1¼ oz.) dry barbecue sauce mix

1 can (1 lb.) tomatoes
1 cup rice
2 cups water
½ cup chopped celery
½ cup chopped green pepper

Coat chicken with flour seasoned with salt and pepper; brown in cooking oil.

Combine remaining ingredients. Pour into greased baking pan (12-by-8 inches); spread chicken over mixture. Cover with piece of aluminum foil, sealing down edges. Bake in preheated oven at 350° for 30 minutes. Uncover; bake another 15 minutes.

Makes 4 servings.

CHICKEN-GREEN BEAN CASSEROLE

3 cups chicken cooked and diced
1 can (10¾ oz.) cream of mushroom soup
1 can (11 oz.) cheddar cheese soup
½ cup milk
1 can (lb.) mixed Chinese vegetables, drained

1 small chopped onion
2 cans (lb.) green beans, drained
1 tsp. salt
⅛ tsp. white pepper
1 can (3½ oz.) French-fried onion rings

Combine ingredients, except onion rings. Place in greased casserole. Bake in preheated 350° oven for 15 minutes.

Top with onion rings; bake another 15 minutes.

Makes 6 servings.

Note: Leftover turkey or roast pork may be substituted for chicken.

FRIED CHICKEN SOUTHERN STYLE

2 frying chickens, cut up
2 cups flour
1 tsp. salt
½ tsp. white pepper
1 cup cooking oil

Wash and dry chicken pieces. Mix flour, salt, and pepper; place in plastic bag. Add chicken and shake to coat.

Add cooking oil to skillet; heat; add chicken. Fry until chicken is brown on both sides, about 45 minutes. Chicken may be cooked covered the first 10 or 15 minutes.

Makes 6-8 servings.

CHICKEN A LA KIEV

4 chicken breasts
2 tbsp. chopped chives (frozen, freeze-dried, or freshly chopped)
4 pats butter or margarine
2 cups flour
2 eggs, beaten
½ cup cream
2 cups bread crumbs or breading mix
1 tsp. salt
¼ tsp. white pepper
4 cups cooked rice

Bone and flatten chicken breasts. Sprinkle with chives; place pat of butter in center. Fold together; secure with round toothpick.

Add cream to beaten eggs; season crumbs with salt and pepper.

Dip breasts in flour, then in egg mixture; roll in breading. Place in greased baking pan in preheated 375° oven for about 30 minutes. Serve over cooked rice.

Makes 4 servings.

CHICKEN A LA KING

2 cups cooked chicken, diced
2 tbsp. butter or margarine
1 green pepper, minced
1 pimento, diced
1 cup sliced mushrooms
2 cups chicken stock
1 pkg. (10 oz.) frozen peas
¼ cup flour mixed with ½ cup water

½ tsp. celery salt
½ tsp. salt
⅛ tsp. white pepper
1 cup cream, sour cream, or evaporated milk
2 egg yolks

In a heavy saucepan, combine butter or margarine, green pepper, pimento, mushrooms, chicken stock, and frozen peas. Cook about 5 minutes; stir in flour; cook until thickened. Add chicken; heat thoroughly. Remove from heat. Add cream mixed with beaten egg yolks. Mix well. Serve immediately.
Makes 6 servings.
Note: Do not boil after adding cream.

CHICKEN LIVERS STROGANOFF

1½ lb. chicken livers
⅓ cup flour
1 tsp. salt
cooking oil
1 cup sour cream
1 can (10¾ oz.) cream of mushroom soup

2 tbsp. minced onion
1 tsp. dill seed
⅓ cup dry white wine or 1 tbsp. vinegar

Pierce livers with kitchen fork to prevent splattering. Halve livers, then shake in bag with flour and salt. Brown livers in cooking oil; remove to bowl.
In a saucepan, combine soup, onion, dill, and wine; heat; add sour cream and livers. Heat about 5 minutes, but do not boil.
Serve over mashed potatoes, hot biscuits, or toast.
Makes 4 servings.

CHICKEN MARENGO

1 (2½-3 lb.) frying chicken, cut up
cooking oil
1 can (1 lb.) tomatoes
1 can (6 oz.) tomato paste
½ cup dry sherry
1 can (6 oz.) sliced mushrooms
1 bay leaf
¼ tsp. garlic powder
1 tsp. salt
1 can (8 oz.) small whole onions
1 cup pitted ripe olives, sliced

Brown chicken in cooking oil. Pour off excess fat. Add all ingredients, except onions and olives to skillet. Cover; cook about 30 minutes. Uncover; add olives and onions; simmer 10 minutes.

Makes 4 servings.

ORIENTAL CHICKEN

1 (2½-3 lb.) chicken or 2 chicken breasts, cooked, boned, and diced
1 green pepper, cut in strips
1 onion, chopped
1 cup chopped celery
1 can (5 oz.) water chestnuts, drained and sliced
4 tbsp. cooking oil
1 cup chicken broth
1 tsp. salt
¼ tsp. white pepper
¼ tsp. ginger
1 tbsp. cornstarch
2 tbsp. soy sauce
1 can (1 lb.) bean sprouts or mixed Chinese vegetables, rinsed and drained
4 cups hot cooked rice or 1 can (5 oz.) Chinese noodles

Heat salad oil in skillet; sauté green pepper, onion, celery, chicken, and water chestnuts a few minutes.

Mix cornstarch with soy sauce; add to skillet. Add remaining ingredients. Simmer about 15 minutes. Serve with hot cooked rice or Chinese noodles.

Makes 4 servings.

OVEN-FRIED PARMESAN CHICKEN

1 (2½-3 lb.) frying chicken, cut up
1 cup crushed herb-seasoned stuffing
⅓ cup grated Parmesan cheese
¼ cup chopped parsley
¼ cup butter or margarine, melted

Combine stuffing, cheese, and parsley. Dip chicken pieces in melted butter or margarine; roll in stuffing mixture. Arrange, skin side up, on greased baking pan. Sprinkle with remaining butter and crumbs. Bake in preheated oven at 375° about 45 minutes.
Makes 4 servings.

CREAM OF CHICKEN AND NOODLES

1 (2½-3 lb.) chicken
water to measure
1 pkg. (12 oz.) noodles
2 cans (10¾ oz.) cream of chicken soup
1 tbsp. salt

Place chicken in pot; add salted water; simmer until done. Remove meat from bones; cube or dice; set aside. Strain broth to remove any bones; measure broth and return to pot, adding enough water to make 8 cups.
Add noodles and bring to boil, forking to separate. Lower heat to simmer. Cook about 15 minutes. Add chicken and soup; salt to taste. Simmer until done.
Makes 12 servings.

CHICKEN WITH NOODLES

1 (2½-3 lb.) chicken
water to measure
1 tbsp. salt
½ tsp. white pepper
1 tbsp. chopped parsley
2 carrots
1 stalk celery, cut in two
1 onion
1 pkg. (12 oz.) noodles
2 tbsp. flour
¼ cup cold water

Place first 8 ingredients in large pot; add water. Cover. Simmer until chicken is tender. Remove meat from bones, cube or dice; set aside.

Remove chicken and vegetables. Strain broth to remove any bones; measure and return to pot, adding enough water to make 8 cups. Place vegetables in blender, or mash or dice and return to pot.

Add noodles and bring to boil. Lower heat to simmer. Cook noodles, forking to separate, about 15 minutes. Mix flour with ¼ cup water; add it and chicken to pot. Simmer until done, about 20 minutes.

Makes 12 servings.

CHICKEN PATTIES

1 (2½-3 lb.) chicken
¾ cup minced onion
1 cup bread crumbs
3 eggs, slightly beaten
1 can (10¾ oz.) cream of chicken soup

1 tsp. salt
⅛ tsp. white pepper
1 cup flour
cooking oil

Boil chicken until tender; remove meat from bones; dice.

Mix chicken, onion, bread crumbs, eggs, and soup together. Shape into patties, then roll in flour seasoned with salt and pepper. Fry on both sides in skillet in hot oil.

Makes 12 patties.

CHICKEN POT PIE

1 (2½-3 lb.) chicken
water
1 small onion, chopped
4 tbsp. flour
2½ cups chicken stock
1 tsp. salt
¼ tsp. white pepper
1 pkg. (10 oz.) frozen peas and carrots, right from freezer

BISCUIT CRUST
2 cups flour
2 tsp. baking powder
1 tsp. salt
½ cup shortening, softened; not melted
1 egg, slightly beaten
¼ cup milk

Chicken and Other Fowl

To make crust: Follow procedure for making baking powder biscuits. Mix and knead dry ingredients and shortening; add egg, then milk. Roll out enough to fit your casserole top. Set aside.

Place chicken in pot with small amount of water. Cook until tender. Remove from pot. Measure and reserve 2½ cups stock. Remove chicken meat from bone; cube.

In a bowl mix cooked chicken with blend of flour, stock, and seasoning. Pour into greased casserole; preferably round. Sprinkle peas and carrots over chicken. Place crust on top. Bake in preheated 425° oven about 30 minutes.

Makes 6 servings.

ROAST CHICKEN

2 (2½-3 lb.) frying chickens
¼ cup melted butter or margarine

stuffing if desired

Wash chickens; stuff and secure with skewers or round toothpicks. Brush with melted butter.

Place on rack in roasting pan. Bake in preheated 375° oven, covered, about 45 minutes. Uncover; bake about 45 more minutes, or until tender.

Makes 4-6 servings.

CHICKEN ROCOCO

4 chicken breasts
1 pkg. (10 oz.) cheddar cheese
2 eggs, beaten
¾ cup dry bread crumbs
⅓ cup cooking oil
1 chicken bouillon cube dissolved in 1 cup boiling water
1 small onion, chopped

1 small green pepper, chopped
2 tbsp. flour
1 tsp. salt
¼ tsp. white pepper
1 can (3 oz.) sliced mushrooms, drained
1 pkg. (6 oz.) white and wild rice mix
2 cups hot water

Mix rice in water and allow to simmer while preparing other ingredients.

Skin, bone, and flatten chicken breasts. Cut each breast in two pieces. Cut cheese in 8 equal strips. Roll each piece of breast around cheese. Secure with round toothpick. Dip roll in egg, then in bread crumbs, and brown in cooking oil. Remove from pan and set aside.

Brown onion and green pepper in skillet; add flour, bouillon dissolved in hot water, and seasonings. Heat until thickened.

Layer cooked rice, mushrooms, and chicken in a baking dish; add onion mixture. Bake in preheated 375° oven for 30 minutes.

Makes 4 servings.

SESAME CHICKEN

6 chicken breasts
½ cup dry vermouth
1 tbsp. soy sauce
½ tsp. powdered ginger
½ lb. fresh mushrooms
6 green onions, cut from root end in 3 or four diagonal pieces
2 tomatoes, cut in wedges
2 tbsp. cooking oil
1 chicken bouillon cube dissolved in ½ cup boiling water
2 tsp. cornstarch
1 tbsp. dry vermouth
2 tbsp. sesame seeds

Remove skin from breasts and bone. Fold together and secure with round toothpick. Combine vermouth, soy sauce, and ginger. Pour over chicken and let stand 1 hour. Drain chicken and pat dry, reserving marinade.

Brown chicken in cooking oil in skillet. Add mushrooms and onions to bouillon, then pour over chicken; cover and simmer about 25 minutes.

Mix cornstarch with the tablespoon of vermouth; stir into pan. Add tomato and cook until sauce is clear. Add sesame seeds. Serve.

Makes 6 servings.

Chicken and Other Fowl

CHICKEN SPAGHETTI

1 (2½-3 lb.) chicken
   water to measure
1 pkg. (8 oz.) elbow spaghetti
1 can (1 lb. 12 oz.) tomatoes
2 green peppers, chopped
2 onions, chopped
2 cups celery, chopped

1 can (11 oz.) cheddar cheese soup
1 can (10¾ oz.) cream of mushroom soup
1 tsp. salt
½ tsp. white pepper

Boil chicken in large pot until tender. Remove from pot; remove bones; cube; set aside. Strain broth to remove any bones; measure and return to pot, adding enough water to make 7 cups.

Put chicken and all other ingredients in pot. Cook about 30 minutes.

Makes 8 servings.

SPANISH CHICKEN AND RICE

1 (2½-3 lb.) frying chicken, cut up
2 tbsp. cooking oil
1 large chopped onion
1 chopped green pepper
1 cup uncooked rice

1 (8 oz.) can tomato sauce with cheese
2 cups water
1 tsp. salt
   dash pepper
1 tbsp. chili powder

Brown chicken in cooking oil; add onion and green pepper, sauté for a few minutes. Stir in rest of ingredients. Cover. Cook slowly about 45 minutes.

Makes 4-6 servings.

FRIED CHICKEN VICHYSSOISE

1 (2½-3 lb.) frying chicken, cut up
⅓ cup flour
1 tsp. salt
1 tsp. paprika
½ cup cooking oil
3 potatoes, peeled and cut in ½-inch thick slices
6 green onions, sliced diagonally from root end to just where green begins

2 chicken bouillon cubes dissolved in 1 cup boiling water
½ tsp. salt
¼ tsp. white pepper
1 cup sour cream

Wash and dry chicken pieces. Mix flour, salt, and paprika in plastic bag. Add chicken and shake to coat.

Add cooking oil to skillet; heat; add chicken. Brown on one side; turn; push to center of pan.

Arrange potato slices around the edge. Sprinkle green onions over top. Add bouillon, salt, and pepper. Cover and simmer for 35 minutes, or until chicken is tender. Remove to serving platter.

Blend sour cream into liquid in skillet; cook and stir until heated through. Pour a little sauce over chicken and potatoes; pass the remainder.

Makes 4 servings.

JACK SPRATT'S PLATTER

On a large platter, arrange slices or pieces of roast chicken or turkey, white meat on one end, and dark meat on the other. In the center, place mashed or small, new, parsleyed potatoes.

On side with white meat, place bowl of white gravy (one-half the quantity of gravy). Add 1 teaspoon of bottled browning and seasoning sauce to remainder of gravy; pour into identical bowl; place beside dark meat.

CORNISH HENS AND WILD RICE

4 Rock Cornish hens, thawed
2 tbsp. margarine or butter
½ cup celery, diced
1 can (4 oz.) sliced mushrooms, drained
1 pkg. (6 oz.) long grain and wild rice combined

1 pkg. (1¼ oz.) onion soup mix
3½ cups hot water
salt
margarine or butter

Place roasting pan on stove burner; melt margarine or butter; add celery, rice, and mushrooms; sauté a few minutes. Combine soup mix with water; pour over rice mixture.

Rub hens with additional margarine or butter and salt. Place in roasting pan; remove to oven. Roast for 30 minutes covered; 30 minutes uncovered in a preheated 375° oven.

Makes 4 servings.

BAKED PHEASANT

1 pheasant, cut into serving pieces
1 cup flour

1 tsp. salt
½ tsp. white pepper
¼ cup cooking oil

Shake pheasant with flour and seasonings in plastic bag. Brown coated parts in cooking oil in skillet. Place in roasting pan in preheated 325° oven for about 1½ hours.

Makes 3 servings.

BAKED PHEASANT WITH RICE

2 pheasants, cut into serving pieces
1 cup flour
½ tsp. salt
¼ tsp. white pepper
½ cup cooking oil
1 cup uncooked rice*

2 cups hot water
1 small onion, grated
1 can (3 oz.) sliced mushrooms
¼ lb. butter or margarine
1 tsp. salt
½ tsp. pepper

Shake pheasant pieces with flour, salt, and pepper in plastic bag. Brown coated parts in cooking oil in skillet. Place rice, hot water, and last five ingredients in roasting pan. Place pheasant pieces on mixture. Bake in preheated 325° oven for about 1½ hours.

Makes 6 servings.

TURKEY HAWAIIAN

3 cups cooked turkey, diced
2 tbsp. margarine or butter
1 pkg. (10 oz.) frozen peas
1½ cups celery, diced
1 can (3 oz.) sliced mushrooms, drained
1 can (lb.) chicken broth
¾ cup water

4 tbsp. soy sauce
1 can (13 oz.) pineapple tidbits
¼ cup cornstarch
1 can (5 oz.) water chestnuts, drained and sliced
4 cups hot cooked rice

In a large saucepan, place margarine, peas, celery, and chicken broth. Cook 5 minutes. Mix cornstarch in the water; add to saucepan and bring to a boil. Add remaining ingredients, turkey last of all. Cover; cook another 10 minutes. Serve over hot cooked rice.

Makes 8 servings.

---

*You may substitute 1 box (6 oz.) wild rice and white rice prepared mixture, than use 2½ cups of water.

TURKEY TETRAZZINI

2 cups cooked turkey, cubed
1 pkg. (8 oz.) elbow spaghetti, 1-inch pieces
1 pkg. (10 oz.) frozen peas
½ tsp. salt
7 cups hot water
1 cup Swiss cheese, grated
¼ cup Parmesan cheese, grated
1 can (10¾ oz.) cream of celery soup
4 tbsp. butter or margarine
4 tbsp. flour
¾ cup powdered milk

Method No. 1: Place spaghetti, peas, salt, and hot water in heavy saucepan. Cook 10 minutes. Mix flour with powdered milk so it will not lump. Add cheese, soup, margarine to pan. Stir in powdered milk and flour. Add turkey. Stir occasionally while cooking another 20 minutes.

Method No. 2: Do not add cheese to pot; cook as above, except for the last 20 minutes. Transfer to casserole dish with Swiss and Parmesan sprinkled over top, and cook in preheated oven at 375° for the 20 minutes.

Makes 8 servings.

5

FISH AND SEAFOOD

CREAMED CODFISH

1 lb. frozen or dried salt codfish
6 tbsp. butter or margarine
6 tbsp. flour
¼ tsp. salt
¼ tsp. white pepper
4 cups hot water
1⅓ cup dry powdered milk

If frozen, thaw codfish. If dried, soak in cold water for 3 hours, changing water every hour.

Shred codfish; cook in hot water about 20 minutes. Mix flour with dry powdered milk, adding salt and pepper. Pour into codfish, stirring until thickened. Serve over toast or hot mashed potatoes.

Makes 4 servings.

CODFISH CAKES

1 lb. frozen or dried salt codfish
3 medium potatoes, peeled and quartered
1 tbsp. butter or margarine
3 tbsp. milk
2 eggs, beaten
½ tsp. salt
½ tsp. white pepper
flour and cooking oil

If frozen, thaw codfish. If dried, soak in cold water for 3 hours, changing water every hour.

Shred codfish; cook with potatoes until potatoes are tender. Use very little water when cooking, so that you can mash potatoes in this water. Add rest of ingredients; beat until fluffy. Shape into patties. Dredge with flour; fry in cooking oil until browned.

Makes 8 patties.

FRIED FISH

In spite of the many ways to prepare fish, they are seldom better than when pan fried, whether whole or a fillet. Use a prepared breading, plain flour, or a mixture of 2 cups flour, 1 cup cornmeal, and 1 tablespoon of salt. If fish are frozen, they may be immediately prepared for cooking by running under the warm water faucet, or by dipping into warm water.

Dip and coat fish with beaten egg, then with the breading; place in hot grease or cooking oil in skillet (or in French fryer at 325° F.) If frying in skillet, lower heat to keep fish barely frying. Brown on one side, then turn so as not to break crust, and brown the other side. In a French fryer, fish are done when they float.

The following fish may be pan or French fried: Bass, Bullheads, Catfish, Carp, Cod fillet, Flounder, Haddock, Perch, Pike, Sole, Trout, Red snapper.

FRESH SALMON BAKED OR GRILLED

1 6 lb. salmon
2 lemons
1 onion
2 bay leaves

SAUCE
¼ cup prepared liquid smoke
2 cups catsup
4 tbsp. butter or margarine
1 tsp. horseradish
1 tsp. celery salt
1 tbsp. salt

A whole salmon may be purchased from the local fish market, or your grocery market will order it for you. A 6-pound salmon will fit on a cookie sheet in your oven, or it may be grilled on an outdoor grill.

Wash salmon. Cut lemons and onion into quarters; put lemons, onion, and bay leaves into cavity of fish.

Place on double layer of aluminum foil on cookie sheet or grill. Bake in preheated 350° oven about 2½ hours. Baking time

Fish and Seafood

is the same on the grill. Baste with sauce. If using grill, pour sauce over salmon before cooking and wrap in foil. Do not unwrap. Prepare another sheet of foil to place under salmon when it is turned about half-way through cooking time. Do not turn if baking in oven. Remove lemon, onion, and bay leaves before serving.

Makes 6 servings.

SALMONBURGERS

1 can (1 lb.) salmon, drained and flaked; reserve liquid
1 small onion, diced
¼ cup cooking oil
½ cup dry bread crumbs
2 eggs, beaten
1 tsp. dry mustard
½ tsp. salt
⅓ cup salad dressing or mayonnaise
1 tbsp. sweet pickle relish
6 hamburger buns, buttered and toasted
flour

Mix salmon, liquid, onion, crumbs, eggs, mustard, and salt in bowl and shape into patties. Lightly flour and brown in cooking oil. Cook brown on each side, then turn and cook a few minutes longer. Mix salad dressing or mayonnaise with sweet pickle relish. Place burgers on bottom half of bun; top with relish mixture and other half of bun.

Makes 6 servings.

SALMON DINNER ROLL

1 can (1 lb.) salmon, flaked
2 cups flour
½ tsp. salt
¼ tsp. pepper
4 tbsp. shortening
1 egg
milk to measure
4 tbsp. milk
2 tbsp. lemon juice
2 tsp. onion, minced
1½ tsp. chopped parsley
½ tsp. salt

Sift together flour, salt, and pepper. Mix in shortening with fork. Beat egg slightly in measuring cup and add enough milk to make ¾ cup. Add to mixture. Roll out dough on floured board in sheet 8 inches long and ¼ inch thick.

Mix salmon, the 4 tablespoons of milk and other remaining ingredients. Spread evenly on dough. Roll up like jelly roll, securing with round toothpicks. Bake on baking sheet in preheated 450° oven for 30 minutes. Slice and serve.

Makes 6 servings.

SALMON LOAF

- 1 can (16 oz.) salmon, flaked
- 1 can (10¾ oz.) cream of celery soup
- 1½ cups soft bread crumbs or cracker meal
- 2 tbsp. sweet pickle relish
- 2 tbsp. lemon juice
- 1 tsp. salt
- ¼ tsp. white pepper
- 2 eggs, beaten

Beat eggs in mixing bowl. Combine all other ingredients. Turn into loaf pan. Bake in preheated oven at 375° about 30 minutes.

Makes 6 servings.

SALMON PARMESAN

- 1 can (1 lb.) salmon, flaked
- ¼ cup shredded Parmesan cheese
- 1 can (10¾ oz.) cream of celery soup
- ½ cup mayonnaise or salad dressing
- ¼ cup milk
- 1 pkg. (10 oz.) frozen peas, cooked
- 1 pkg. (8 oz.) noodles, cooked and drained
- 1 tsp. onion, minced

Combine first five ingredients; mix well. Stir in peas, noodles, and onion. Pour into casserole. Bake in preheated 350° oven about 30 minutes.

Makes 6 servings.

Fish and Seafood

SALMON PATTIES

1 can (16 oz.) salmon, flaked
1 can (10¾ oz.) cream of celery soup
1½ cups soft bread crumbs or cracker meal
2 tbsp. lemon juice
1 tsp. salt
¼ tsp. white pepper
2 eggs, beaten
6 tbsp. flour
cooking oil

Beat eggs in bowl. Combine all other ingredients. Shape into patties. Brown on both sides in a small amount of cooking oil in skillet.
Makes 6 patties.

SALMON PUFF

1 can (1 lb.) salmon, flaked
3 tbsp. butter or margarine
3 tbsp. flour
1 tsp. salt
½ tsp. dry mustard
½ tsp. Worcestershire sauce
1 cup milk
4 eggs, separated

In medium saucepan over low heat, melt butter or margarine; stir in flour, salt, mustard, and Worcestershire sauce until blended. Slowly stir in milk, and cook, stirring constantly, until thickened; cool about 10 minutes. Beat in egg yolks, one at a time. Stir salmon into mixture.
In large bowl, beat egg whites until stiff; fold gently into mixture. Pour into greased casserole. Bake about 45 minutes in preheated 350° oven.
Makes 6 servings.
Note: Be sure oven is hot when mixture is placed in oven.

CREAMED SMOKED SALMON

½ lb. smoked salmon, flaked
½ cup flour
4 tbsp. butter or margarine
3 cups milk or 3 cups water and 1 cup dry powdered milk

Melt butter or margarine in saucepan. Remove from heat; stir in flour. Add milk and salmon, then return to heat. Cook, stirring constantly, until thickened. Taste before adding salt. Serve over mashed potatoes or toast.

Makes 4 servings.

TUNA BARBECUE

- 2 cans (7 oz. each) tuna
- ½ cup chopped onion
- 2 tbsp. cooking oil
- ½ cup chopped celery
- ½ cup chopped green pepper
- 1 cup catsup
- 1 cup water
- 2 tbsp. brown sugar
- 2 tbsp. vinegar
- 2 tbsp. Worcestershire sauce
- 1 tsp. prepared mustard
- ½ tsp. salt
- ⅛ tsp. white pepper

Sauté onion, celery, and green pepper in cooking oil until limp. Add remaining ingredients, except tuna. Simmer for 20 minutes. Add tuna (broken into big pieces). Heat thoroughly. Serve.

Makes 6 servings.

TUNA-BROCCOLI

- 1 pkg. (10 oz.) frozen broccoli
- ¼ cup water
- 1 can (7 oz.) tuna
- 1 can (10¾ oz.) cream of mushroom soup
- ½ cup milk
- 1 bag (1⅛ oz.) potato chips, crushed
- 2 hard-boiled eggs, sliced

Cook broccoli in water for 4 minutes. Drain. Place in 8-by-11-inch baking pan. Cover with tuna. Add eggs, soup, and milk. Sprinkle crushed chips on top. Bake for 30 minutes in 375° preheated oven.

Makes 4 servings.

Fish and Seafood

CHEESE AND TUNA CASSEROLE

2 cans (7 oz. each) tuna, drained and flaked; reserve liquid
1 can (1 lb.) cut green beans, drained
3 tbsp. flour
1 pkg. (8 oz.) shredded cheddar cheese
1 can (3½ oz.) French-fried onion rings
1 can (10¾ oz.) cream of mushroom soup
1 cup tuna liquid and milk
1 tsp. seasoned salt
1 tube (10) prepared biscuits

In casserole, layer beans, tuna, cheese, and half the onions; add remaining ingredients, except biscuits. Place in preheated 400° oven for 10 minutes. Remove casserole from oven; place biscuits around top; bake for 12 minutes; add remaining onion rings in center; bake 3 minutes longer.
Makes 6 servings.

CURRIED TUNA

2 cans (7 oz. each) tuna
1 small onion, minced
¼ cup flour
2 tsp. curry powder
1 tsp. salt
¼ tsp. ginger
2 cups milk
½ cup chopped toasted almonds
1 tbsp. lemon juice
4 cups hot cooked rice

Drain oil from tuna into saucepan; add onion, and sauté a few minutes. Blend flour, curry powder, salt, and ginger into tuna mixture. Add milk gradually, stirring constantly, until mixture thickens. Add toasted almonds, lemon juice. Simmer a few minutes; spoon over hot cooked rice.
Makes 6 servings.

TUNA DELIGHT

2 cans (7 oz. each) tuna, drained and flaked
2 eggs, separated
½ tsp. salt
¼ tsp. white pepper
2 cups soft bread crumbs
1½ cups mayonnaise or salad dressing
1 pkg. (10 oz.) frozen peas and carrots, cooked
1 green pepper, chopped
2 tbsp. diced onion
2 cups mashed potatoes
2 tbsp. butter or margarine, melted

In a large bowl, beat egg yolks; blend in salt and pepper, crumbs, 1 cup of the mayonnaise, vegetables (except mashed potatoes), and tuna. Place in casserole; smooth top. Bake in preheated 350° oven about 25 minutes.

Meanwhile, beat egg whites until stiff peaks form; fold in remaining mayonnaise.

Remove casserole from oven; spread egg-white mixture in center of top of casserole; place potatoes as border. Brush potatoes with melted butter. Return casserole to oven for about 15 minutes.

Makes 6 servings.

FISH 'N' CHIPS CASSEROLE

2 cans (7 oz. each) tuna
3 tbsp. butter or margarine
3 tbsp. flour
½ tsp. salt
⅛ tsp. celery seed
⅛ tsp. white pepper
1½ cups milk
1 pkg. (10 oz.) frozen chopped asparagus, cooked and drained
1 pimento, sliced (optional)
1 cup grated Swiss cheese
1 pkg. (4 oz.) potato chips, crumbled

Melt butter in saucepan; blend in flour; gradually add milk, and cook until sauce boils. Add seasonings. Put asparagus, tuna, pimento in casserole; pour cooked mixture over it; top with cheese and chips. Bake in preheated 350° oven about 20 minutes.

Makes 6 servings.

TUNA FLORENTINE

2 cans (7 oz. each) tuna, drained; reserve liquid
1 pkg. (10 oz.) frozen chopped spinach, cooked and drained
3 tbsp. flour
½ tsp. salt
1½ cups milk
½ cup shredded Swiss cheese
½ cup light cream
⅛ tsp. white pepper

Drain oil from tuna into saucepan; blend in flour; add milk and seasonings. Cook over low heat until mixture thickens. Add shredded cheese and cream, stirring until cheese is melted.
Place spinach and tuna in casserole; pour mixture over it. Bake in preheated 350° oven about 20 minutes.
Makes 6 servings.

TUNA ITALIANO

1 can (7 oz.) tuna
1 pkg. (8 oz.) macaroni
6 cups boiling water
1 small chopped onion
1 small chopped green pepper
2 slices cheddar cheese
1 tbsp. butter or margarine
1 can (10¾ oz.) mushroom soup
1 can (10¾ oz.) tomato soup
½ tsp. white pepper
1 tsp. salt
1 tsp. grated Parmesan cheese

To boiling water in a saucepan, add macaroni, onion, and green pepper. Cook until macaroni is tender. Mix and blend in remaining ingredients. Simmer about 10 minutes.
Makes 4 servings.

TUNA JAMBALAYA

2 cans (9¼ oz. each) tuna
1 can (1 lb.) stewed tomatoes
2 cans (8 oz. each) tomato sauce
2 sauce cans water
1 tsp. salt
½ tsp. chili powder
¼ tsp. white pepper
1 pkg. (6 oz.) white and wild rice
2 cups hot water

Combine ingredients in saucepan. Bring to boil; cover and simmer about 30 minutes.

Makes 8 servings.

TUNA-NOODLES WITH CHEDDAR CHEESE

2 cans (7 oz. each) tuna
1 pkg. (8 oz.) noodles
1 pkg. (1½ oz.) spaghetti sauce mix
1 can (1 lb. 12 oz.) tomatoes
1 tsp. seasoned salt
1½ cups shredded cheddar cheese
6 cups hot water

Place ingredients in heavy saucepan. Stir well. Cook about 25 minutes.

Makes 8 servings.

TUNA ROMANOFF

2 cans (7 oz. each) tuna
1 pkg. (8 oz.) noodles, cooked
1 cup cottage cheese
1 cup sour cream
2 tbsp. minced onion
2 tbsp. chopped pimento
2 tbsp. lemon juice
1 tbsp. Worcestershire sauce
4 drops Tabasco sauce
½ cup pitted ripe olives, sliced
1 tsp. salt
¼ tsp. white pepper

Place noodles in bottom of greased casserole. Mix remaining ingredients; pour over noodles. Bake in preheated 350° oven for 45 minutes.

Makes 8 servings.

TUNA STROGANOFF

2 cans (7 oz. each) tuna
1 pkg. (8 oz.) noodles, cooked
½ tsp. salt
¼ tsp. white pepper
1 cup sour cream
½ cup milk
1 can (10¾ oz.) cream of mushroom soup
1 pkg. (10 oz.) frozen peas
⅓ cup diced celery
⅓ cup minced onion
½ cup bread crumbs
2 tbsp. melted margarine or butter

Fish and Seafood

Place cooked noodles in bottom of casserole. Layer tuna and peas. Combine remaining ingredients, except last two. Pour mixture in casserole. Garnish with bread crumbs and margarine. Bake uncovered in preheated oven at 350° for 45 minutes.

Makes 8 servings.

TUNA TETRAZZINI

7 cups hot water
2 cans (7 oz. each) tuna
1 pkg. (8 oz.) elbow spaghetti
1 can (10¾ oz.) cream of celery soup
1 cup milk
1 can (10¾ oz.) cream of mushroom soup
1 onion, chopped fine
¼ cup pitted ripe olives, sliced
1 cup shredded cheddar cheese

Place hot water in heavy saucepan; add ingredients; bring to boiling point, stirring occasionally. Turn down heat, simmer about 30 minutes.

Makes 8 servings.

STEAMED CLAMS

36 Little Neck clams
⅛ lb. butter
juice of ½ lemon
2 cups water
salt
white pepper

Soak clams in cold water in refrigerator overnight. Scrub the shell with a vegetable brush. Rinse several times.

Place on rack in cooking pan; add water. Cover pan. Steam about 8 minutes or until clams open. Discard any that do not open.

Melt butter; add lemon juice, salt, and pepper. Remove clams from pan to serving dish; add butter mixture to broth; heat a minute, and pour mixture into consomme cups in equal portions.

Note: The tough part, known as the neck, is not eaten.

CHEDDAR-CRAB CASSEROLE

2 cans (7½ oz. each) crab meat, drained and flaked; reserve liquid
⅛ lb. butter or margarine
½ cup celery, chopped
¼ cup onion, chopped
¼ cup green pepper, chopped
¼ cup flour
2 cups cooked rice, cold
2 cups cheddar cheese, shredded

1 can (4 oz.) sliced mushrooms, drained
⅓ cup pitted ripe olives, sliced
¼ cup slivered almonds
2 tbsp. butter or margarine, melted
⅛ cup dry bread crumbs
1 tsp. salt
2 cups milk

In a saucepan, melt butter; sauté celery, onion, and green pepper. Blend in flour and salt. Remove from heat; gradually add milk; return to heat; cook, stirring constantly, until mixture thickens.

In a large bowl, combine remaining ingredients, except 2 tablespoons of butter and bread crumbs. Add cooked mixture. Turn into greased casserole.

Sprinkle bread crumbs and butter over top. Bake in preheated oven at 350° for 45 minutes.

Makes 6 servings.

BASIC DIRECTIONS FOR COOKING SOUTH AFRICAN ROCK LOBSTER TAILS*

How to broil in the whole shell:

Thaw tails. Hold the shell in palm of one hand; insert point of pair of kitchen shears between the hard upper shell and the soft underside membrane. Snip down each side and lift the membrane off. Grasp tail in both hands and crack the shell firmly lengthwise. This cracking makes the shells lie flat during

---

*"South African Rock Lobster Tails" is a brand name. Other brands may be substituted.

Fish and Seafood

broiling. Preheat broiler 10 minutes; place shell side up, 4 inches below heat. Broil tails according to timetable, turning as indicated. Serve in shell with melted butter.

How to boil:

Drop tails, either thawed or frozen, into large kettle of boiling water with teaspoon salt for each quart. When water reboils, lower heat and begin counting time, following timetable. Drain immediately and drench with cold water. Cut away underside membrane with kitchen shears. Insert fingers between shell and meat at heavy end of tail, work meat loose from shell. Meat can be removed easily in one solid piece.

How to bake:

Wrap each tail securely in heavy duty aluminum foil. If tails are thawed, cut away underside membrane. Place in baking pan; bake in preheated oven at 450°, according to timetable. Remove from oven and loosen foil. If tails were frozen at start, remove underside membrane after baking with kitchen shears, being sure to hold tails with an oven mitt. Serve with melted butter.

How to deep fry:

Drop tails into boiling salted water and cook only until water reboils, just enough to parboil the tails and facilitate removal from shell. Drain immediately, drench with cold water, and cut away underside membrane with kitchen shears. Insert fingers between shell and meat at heavy end of tail, and work meat loose from shell. Meat can be removed easily in one solid piece. Roll meat in egg batter and then lightly in breading mix. Melt shortening in deep pan and heat slowly until a tiny wisp of steam arises. In a basket or with slotted spoon, gently lower breaded tails into hot fat and cook until golden brown. When tails are done, drain on absorbent paper and serve immediately.

How to prepare "Piggy Back":

Thaw tails. Insert point of kitchen shears between meat and hard shell on back. Clip hard shell down the center, leaving tail "fan" intact. Do not remove underside membrane. Gently open shell, separating it from the meat. Lift raw tail meat through split shell, to rest on outside of shell, leaving meat attached to fan end of shell. Preheat broiler and arrange shells, with meat riding "piggy back" on top, in shallow broiler pan. Brush with melted butter or any desired sauce and broil about 4 inches from heat, following timetable. Brush tails occasionally with additional butter. Tails are done when meat has lost its translucency and is creamy white and opaque. Serve with melted butter.

How to barbecue:

If tails are thawed, cut underside of membrane around edge and remove. Grasp tail in both hands and crack shell firmly lengthwise, to prevent curling. Place tails flesh side toward heat first and grill according to timetable. Turn, brush with butter, and continue grilling until done.

If tails are frozen, cut tails down through middle of hard shell with sharp knife. Cut through flesh but not underside membrane. Grasp tail in both hands and open flat, butterfly style. Place tails flesh side toward heat and barbecue for 5 minutes. Turn tails, brush with butter, and continue grilling, flesh side up according to timetable.

How to cook in microwave oven:

Note carefully weight of lobster. If lobster tails are frozen, unwrap and place in glass cooking dish. Heat 10 seconds per ounce of weight. Let stand at room temperature about 10 minutes to thaw. Make a cut lengthwise down back through hard shell; hold tail in both hands and open flat. Turn tails, meat side up in dish; brush with melted butter and lemon juice. Cook again 10 seconds per ounce of weight. Serve with melted butter.

TIMETABLE FOR COOKING
SOUTH AFRICAN ROCK LOBSTER TAILS*

Weight:	2 oz.	3 oz.	4 oz.	5 oz.	6 oz.	7 oz.	8 oz.
BOILING†							
Frozen	2	3	5	6	8	9	11
Thawed	2	3	4	4	5	6	8
BAKING							
Frozen	20	25	30	35	40	45	50
Thawed	12	15	18	20	22	24	26
BROILING							
Thawed							
(Shell side)	3	4	5	5	5	5	5
(Flesh side)	2	3	3	4	6	7	8
Frozen							
(Butterfly style)	8	10	12	15	17	18	20
Thawed							
(Piggy-Back)	6	8	10	12	14	16	18
BARBECUING‡							
Thawed							
(Flesh side)	4	4	5	6	7	7	8
(Shell side)	5	8	12	15	17	20	22
Frozen							
(Flesh side)	5	5	5	5	5	5	5
(Shell side)	7	9	11	13	17	20	23

---

* In minutes.
† Begin to time after water reboils.
‡ Standard guide under ideal conditions. On outdoor barbecues, heat varies according to size of fire, wind, distance from heat, etc. When lobster loses its translucency, it is done.

CURRIED SOUTH AFRICAN ROCK LOBSTER TAILS

12 (2 oz. each) South African Rock Lobster Tails
¼ cup butter or margarine
3 small onions, diced
¼ tsp. garlic powder
¼ tsp. ground ginger
3 tomatoes, peeled and diced
2 tbsp. curry powder
1 cinnamon stick
1 bay leaf
3 cloves
1 tsp. salt

Parboil frozen rock lobster tails by dropping them into boiling salted water. When water reboils, drain immediately and drench with cold water. Reserving shells for serving, cut away underside membrane; remove meat and dice. Set aside.

Heat butter in heavy pan; add onions and sauté until soft. Add tomatoes and all the seasonings; simmer 30 minutes.

Remove cinnamon stick, bay leaf, and cloves. Add lobster. Heat very slowly, stirring occasionally so that all pieces of lobster are coated with mixture. Heat thoroughly. Replace mixture in reserved shells and serve immediately.

Makes 6 servings.

FONDUE WITH ROCK LOBSTER

18 oz. South African Rock Lobster Tails, any size
1 lb. Swiss cheese
¼ cup white wine
2 tbsp. brandy or Kirsch
French bread cut into cubes

Follow basic directions for boiling lobster according to size selected. When cooked, drench with cold water; drain. Cut away underside membrane; remove meat from shells. Chill. Cut lobster into cubes.

Slice cheese into chafing dish; cover with wine and let stand for an hour. Turn burner to very low heat until cheese melts; add brandy or Kirsch, stirring constantly.

To serve: Spear cubes of lobster and bread with a fondue fork, and dip in fondue to coat with mixture.

Makes 6 servings.

SOUTH AFRICAN ROCK LOBSTER NEWBURG

24 oz. South African Rock Lobster Tails, any size
3 tbsp. butter or margarine
5 tbsp. flour
1½ cups light cream
3 tbsp. dry sherry
2 egg yolks

1 can (4 oz.) sliced mushrooms, drained
½ tsp. salt
⅛ tsp. white pepper
12 slices white bread, toasted just before serving entree

Follow basic directions for boiling lobster according to size selected. When cooked, drench with cold water; drain. Cut away underside membrane; remove meat from shells; cut into ½-inch pieces.

In top of double boiler, melt butter; stir in flour and egg yolks; gradually stir in cream and sherry. Cook until mixture thickens. Stir in lobster, mushrooms, salt and pepper. Heat thoroughly. Serve over toast.

Makes 6 servings.

LOBSTER THERMIDOR

2 pkgs. (8 oz. each) South African Rock Lobster Tails
¼ cup butter or margarine
1 cup mushrooms, fresh or canned, sliced
2 tbsp. flour
¼ tsp. paprika

½ tsp. salt
dash white pepper
½ cup milk
½ cup light cream
1 tbsp. dry sherry
paprika
Parmesan cheese

Boil lobster tails according to directions; drain and cool. Cut membrane. Lift meat out of shells and reserve shells. Dice lobster meat. Melt butter in saucepan; sauté mushrooms a few minutes. Remove from heat. Blend in flour, seasonings, milk, and cream; cook over moderate heat just until thickened. Add sherry; fold lobster into sauce, then spoon mixture into lobster shells. Sprinkle with paprika and Parmesan cheese. Broil about 4 minutes.

Makes 2 servings.

FRENCH-FRIED OYSTERS

1 pint extra select oysters	cracker meal
2 eggs, beaten	cooking oil
1 cup flour	

Dip oysters in flour, then in beaten eggs; roll in cracker meal, and place on wax paper. Chill in refrigerator or freezer for at least ½ hour before frying. French fry at 350°.
Makes 4 servings.

SCALLOPED OYSTERS

2 pints oysters, drained; reserve liquor	1 tsp. minced onion
To oyster liquor, add and mix together:	1 tsp. salt
	dash white pepper
3 cups cracker meal or bread crumbs	dash seasoned salt
	½ cup cream
1 tbsp. melted butter	2 eggs, slightly beaten

In greased baking pan, layer ½ of the crumb mixture. Spread oysters over crumb mixture. Top with remainder of mixture. Bake in preheated oven for 30 minutes.
Makes 8 servings.

SCALLOPED OYSTERS AND CORN

1 pint oysters	1 egg, slightly beaten
1 can (1 lb.) cream-style corn	½ tsp. salt
1 can (1 lb.) whole kernel corn, drained	½ tsp. white pepper
	¼ cup butter, melted
1 cup cracker crumbs	

Combine all ingredients in mixing bowl, except crumbs and butter. Pour into greased casserole; combine crumbs and butter; sprinkle around edges of mixture. Bake in preheated 350° oven about 45 minutes.
Makes 8 servings.

BARBECUED SHRIMP

1 lb. shrimp, cooked
1 small onion, minced
1 small green pepper, chopped
1 cup celery, thinly sliced
3 cups canned tomatoes
1 pkg. (1½ oz.) barbecue sauce mix

½ tsp. seasoned salt
½ tsp. salt
⅛ tsp. white pepper
4 tbsp. cooking oil
4 cups hot cooked rice

Cook onion, green pepper, and celery in cooking oil until tender. Stir in remaining ingredients.

Prepare rice. Let shrimp mixture simmer while rice is cooking. Serve over rice.

Makes 4 servings.

SHRIMP CANTONESE

1 lb. shrimp, cooked and sliced lengthwise
2 cups rice, uncooked (either long grain and wild rice blended, or white rice)
2 tbsp. butter or margarine
2 cups celery, sliced
2 onions, chopped
2 cans (1 lb.) fancy Chinese vegetables, drained and rinsed

¼ tsp. white pepper
¼ cup soy sauce
2 cups chicken broth
2¼ cups water
2 tbsp. cornstarch
1 pkg. (10 oz.) frozen chopped broccoli

Place rice, celery, onion, chicken broth, and 2 cups of the water in heavy pan with cover. Cook about 10 minutes. Add broccoli; cook another 10 minutes. Mix cornstarch in remaining water; add it along with all other ingredients. Cook for another 10 minutes. Simmer until ready to serve, or serve immediately.

Makes 4 servings.

SHRIMP CREOLE

1½ lb. shrimp, cooked
Creole Sauce (*see* Index)

Saffron Rice (*see* Index)

Add shrimp to Creole Sauce; spoon over Saffron Rice Ring. Makes 6 servings.

6

VEGETABLES

CALICO BEANS*

2 cans of each of the following beans:
   green beans, drained
   butter beans, drained and rinsed
   kidney beans, drained and rinsed
   pork and beans

½ lb. thick-sliced bacon
2 medium onions, diced
1½ cup brown sugar
2 tbsp. seasoned salt

Lay bacon on cutting board, cut crosswise in ½-inch pieces. Fry in skillet or large saucepan until bacon bends but doesn't break. Add onion; sauté a few minutes. Add all other ingredients. Heat to boiling.

The beans may be served immediately, stored in refrigerator, or frozen.

Makes 24 servings.

---

* This is our famous Calico Beans that we've served on our salad bar for over ten years. We used thousands of cans of beans, gave the recipe to hundreds of people, and received (it seems) a million compliments.

BAKED BEANS

2 lbs. navy or great northern beans	12 strips bacon
14 cups water	½ cup brown sugar
1 large onion, chopped	½ cup molasses
2 cups catsup	2 tbsp. salt
1 tbsp. Worcestershire sauce	1 tsp. white pepper

Wash beans; place in cooking pan with 8 cups of the water. Bring to boil; set aside to soak overnight or several hours. Rinse. Add about 6 cups water; simmer two hours.

Cut bacon into ½-inch pieces, and brown in skillet, adding onion when half done. Add remaining ingredients. Place in casserole in preheated oven; bake at 350° for 1½ hours. Or simmer on stove for 1 hour, baking the last ½ hour.

Makes 16 servings.

EASY BAKED BEANS

3 cans (16 oz. each) pork and beans in tomato sauce	8 slices bacon
1 small onion, chopped	¼ cup brown sugar
1 cup catsup	½ cup molasses
2 tsp. Worcestershire sauce	2 tsp. salt

Cut bacon in ½-inch pieces and brown in skillet with onion; add remaining ingredients.

Turn into casserole; bake in preheated 350° oven for 45 minutes. Or bring to boiling point, lower heat, and simmer on top of stove for 45 minutes.

Makes 12 servings.

FRENCH GREEN BEANS

1 can (1 lb.) French-style green beans
⅓ cup milk
1 can (10¾ oz.) cream of mushroom soup
1 can (3½ oz.) French-fried onion rings

Combine ingredients (reserving one-half of the onion rings) in casserole. Bake 25 minutes in preheated oven at 350°. Add remaining onion rings; bake 5 minutes longer.
Makes 6 servings.

GREEN BEAN FRITTERS

1 can (1 lb.) French-style green beans
½ tsp. baking powder
¾ cup flour
½ tsp. salt
¼ tsp. white pepper
1 egg, separated
½ cup milk
oil for frying

Drain beans; spread on paper towel to dry. Blend together baking powder, flour, and seasonings. Beat in egg yolk and milk. Add beans. Beat egg white until stiff; fold into mixture. Drop by teaspoons into hot fat (375°); fry until golden brown. Remove with slotted spoon; drain on paper towels.
Makes 24 fritters.

GREEN BEANS ITALIANO

2 cans (1 lb. each) cut green beans, drained
2 tbsp. cooking oil
2 tbsp. wine vinegar
2 tsp. crumbled oregano
¼ tsp. garlic salt
½ cup pitted ripe olives, halved

Heat ingredients in a saucepan. Serve hot.
Makes 8 servings.

PENNSYLVANIA DUTCH-STYLE GREEN BEANS

1 can (1 lb.) cut green beans, drained; reserve ½ cup liquid
3 strips bacon, cooked, drained and crumbled
1 small onion, sliced
2 tsp. cornstarch
¼ tsp. salt
¼ tsp. dry mustard
1 tbsp. brown sugar
1 tbsp. vinegar
1 hard-cooked egg, peeled and sliced

Cook bacon and set aside. Drain off all but 1 tbsp. drippings, then add onion and brown lightly. Mix cornstarch with the liquid from beans; add to onions. Blend in seasonings; add beans and heat thoroughly. Turn into serving dish. Garnish with bacon and sliced egg.

Makes 6 servings.

BEANS AND SPROUTS

1 can (1 lb.) green beans, drained
1 can (1 lb.) bean sprouts, rinsed and drained
1 can (5 oz.) water chestnuts, drained and sliced
1 can (10¾ oz.) mushroom soup
1 can (3 oz.) French-fried onion rings or Chinese noodles

In a casserole, mix all ingredients together except onion rings. Top with onion rings or noodles. Bake in preheated 375° oven for 20 minutes.

Makes 12 servings.

GREEN BEANS SUPREME

2 cans (1 lb. each) cut green beans
1 small onion, sliced
2 tbsp. butter or margarine
2 tbsp. flour
1 tsp. salt
¼ tsp. white pepper
1 tsp. grated lemon peel
1 tbsp. chopped parsley
1 cup sour cream
½ cup shredded cheddar cheese
2 tbsp. butter or margarine, melted
½ cup dried bread crumbs or bran flakes

Cook onion in butter or margarine until barely tender. Add flour and seasonings; stir. Add beans; heat through, then remove from stove and stir in sour cream.

Place mixture in greased casserole. Sprinkle with cheese and buttered crumbs. Broil or bake in oven until cheese melts.

Makes 8 servings.

GREEN BEANS AND WATER CHESTNUTS

2 cans (1 lb. each) green beans, drained
2 tbsp. butter or margarine

1 can (5 oz.) water chestnuts, drained and sliced
½ tsp. seasoned salt

Place ingredients in saucepan. Heat thoroughly.
Makes 8 servings.

SPANISH LIMA BEANS

1 cup dried lima beans or 1 can (lb.) lima beans
5 cups water
6 slices bacon, cut in half-inch pieces
2-3 small onions, sliced

1 can (6 oz.) tomato sauce
½ tsp. salt
¼ tsp. white pepper
½ tsp. paprika
2 tbsp. flour
2 bay leaves

Soak beans overnight in cold water. Rinse; in 5 cups water, simmer for 2 hours.

Fry bacon in skillet; add onions and brown. Add flour and stir; add remaining ingredients except beans. Cook for a few minutes, then add beans and heat thoroughly.

Makes 6 servings.

DUTCH BEETS

1 bunch 6 or 8 beets	1 small onion, minced
2 tbsp. butter or margarine	2 tbsp. vinegar
1 tbsp. flour	½ tsp. salt
1 cup very hot water	⅛ tsp. white pepper
1 tbsp. sugar	

Boil beets in skins until tender. Peel and slice in thick slices. Tops that are good may be reserved and served in mixture with beets.

Melt butter; sauté onion 1 minute, then stir in flour and seasonings; add water and beets. Simmer (do not boil) for 10 minutes.

Makes 4 servings.

HARVARD BEETS I

2 cups beets, cooked, peeled and cut in ½-inch cubes or 1 can (lb.) beets, drained; reserve 2 tbsp. liquid. Cut into ½-inch cubes	⅓ cup sugar 2 tbsp. cornstarch ½ cup sweet cider vinegar 2 tbsp. butter or margarine ½ tsp. salt

Prepare beets. Blend beet liquid with cornstarch for color and mix with other ingredients. Bring just barely to boil. Add beets. Let stand, covered, over low heat ½ hour.

Makes 6 servings.

HARVARD BEETS II

2 cups beets, cooked and diced	1 tbsp. vinegar
2 tbsp. cornstarch	2 tbsp. orange juice
4 tsp. sugar	½ cup liquid from beets
¾ tsp. salt	

Place everything except beets in saucepan. Bring mixture to a boil. Add beets, and let stand, covered, over low heat ½ hour before serving.

Makes 6 servings.

Vegetables

BEET-ONION CASSEROLE

1 bunch 6 or 8 beets
6 small onions, sliced
1 small green pepper, diced
¾ cup sour cream
1 tbsp. lemon juice

½ tsp. seasoned salt
¼ cup water
2 tbsp. butter or margarine
1 cup bread crumbs or bran flakes

Cook beets just until tender enough to remove skins easily. Peel and slice the same thickness as onion, then layer in casserole with onion.

Mix next five ingredients. Pour over beets. Top with crumb mixture and dot with butter. Bake in preheated 350° oven 1 hour.

Makes 8 servings.

BAKED BROCCOLI

1 lb. broccoli
1 cup rice
4 tbsp. butter or margarine
1 can (10¾ oz.) cream of chicken soup
1 soup can milk

1 can (11 oz.) cheddar cheese soup
1 tsp. salt
¼ tsp. white pepper
1 cup bran flakes or 1 pkg. (1⅛ oz.) potato chips

Combine broccoli and rice and simmer with 1½ cups water for about 10 minutes. Combine all ingredients in saucepan except bran flakes or chips. Pour into casserole and top with flakes or chips. Bake in preheated 350° oven 30 minutes.

Makes 6 servings.

BROCCOLI-CAULIFLOWER-CELERY

1 pkg. (10 oz.) frozen broccoli
1 pkg. (10 oz.) frozen cauliflower
1 can (10¾ oz.) cream of celery soup

1 tsp. salt
¼ tsp. white pepper

Cook broccoli (5 minutes) in amount of water as per instructions on box. Add cauliflower, adding only half the amount of water as per instructions. Cook 5 more minutes; add soup and seasonings. Cook 5 additional minutes. Serve.

Makes 8 servings.

BRUSSELS SPROUTS

1 qt. brussels sprouts   2 cups water

Cut off stem ends; wash; remove wilted leaves. Soak in slightly salted water about ½ hour. Drain.

Cook about 20 minutes in boiling water; drain and butter. Taste for saltiness.

Makes 6 servings.

Note: Brussels sprouts may be cooked as above, then creamed in cheese or white sauce. Or they may be cooked with 1 small onion sliced, 3 tablespoons butter or margarine, and a bouillon cube dissolved in cooking water.

CABBAGE AU GRATIN

1 head cabbage, chopped or shredded
4 cups water
½ tsp. salt
¾ cup dry bread crumbs

⅛ tsp. white pepper
1 egg, beaten
2 tbsp. butter or margarine
1½ cups grated cheese
1½ cups milk

Cook cabbage in water about 10 minutes; drain. Beat eggs, milk, and seasonings together. Layer cabbage in casserole with egg mixture and remaining ingredients, reserving some of the crumbs and cheese for topping. Dot with butter and bake in preheated 350° oven about 30 minutes.

Makes 6 servings.

RED CABBAGE WITH APPLES

1 head red cabbage, chopped into ½-inch pieces
4 tbsp. bacon drippings or butter or margarine
2 tart apples, washed, cored, and sliced

½ cup sweet cider vinegar
½ cup water
¼ tsp. ground allspice
4 tbsp. brown sugar
1 tsp. salt

Melt shortening, add sliced apples. Place cabbage on top of apples. Add vinegar, water, allspice, and salt. Cover, cook over medium heat about 30 minutes. Add brown sugar, cook a few more minutes.
Makes 6 servings.

DUTCH-STYLE RED CABBAGE

1 head red cabbage, cut into ¼-inch slices
1 can (1 lb.) sliced pickled beets
¼ tsp. onion salt

⅛ tsp. ground cloves
¼ cup sweet cider vinegar
1 tsp. salt
1 tbsp. sugar

Place cabbage in skillet; add juice from beets. While beets are in can, cut with sharp knife into julienne strips. Add to cabbage. Add seasonings, except sugar. Cover; cook about 45 minutes. Add sugar. Serve.
Makes 6 servings.

CABBAGE HOLLAND STYLE

1 head cabbage, either green or red, chopped into 1-inch pieces
1 small onion, minced
1 tbsp. butter or margarine

1 tsp. salt
2 tbsp. vinegar
⅛ tsp. mace
2 tsp. sugar
¼ tsp. white pepper

Place all ingredients except sugar in skillet; cover. Simmer about 45 minutes. Stir in sugar. Serve hot or cold.
Makes 6 servings.

SCALLOPED CABBAGE WITH CHEESE

1 head cabbage, shredded
1 qt. water
¼ cup margarine
2 tbsp. flour or cornstarch
½ tsp. salt
½ tsp. seasoned salt
¼ tsp. white pepper
¼ tsp. nutmeg (optional)
2 cups milk
½ cup chopped walnuts (optional)
1 cup shredded cheese
2 tbsp. fine dry bread crumbs

Cook cabbage in boiling water 7 minutes; drain. Melt margarine in saucepan; blend in flour or cornstarch. Add milk; heat until mixture thickens.

Place cabbage in casserole; add nuts; pour sauce over cabbage and top with cheese and crumbs. Bake until bubbly.

Makes 6 servings.

SIMMERED RED CABBAGE

1 head red cabbage, shredded
2 tbsp. cooking oil
1 small onion, sliced
1 tart apple, diced
½ cup raisins
½ tsp. ground cloves
½ tsp. allspice
1 tsp. salt
1 tbsp. sugar
1 tbsp. wine vinegar or sweet cider vinegar

Heat oil in saucepan; add cabbage, then add next 5 ingredients. Cover; simmer about 1 hour. Add last 3 ingredients. Serve.

Makes 6 servings.

STEWED CABBAGE

1 head cabbage, either green or red, chopped
4 cups water
2 tbsp. butter or margarine
1 onion, chopped
2 tart apples, cored and chopped
1 tsp. salt
1 stalk celery, chopped
1 sprig parsley (optional)
¼ cup grape juice for red cabbage

Vegetables 111

Place all ingredients, except grape juice in saucepan. Cover, simmer for about 45 minutes. Just before serving, pour in grape juice and stir.
Makes 6 servings.

SWEET-SOUR CABBAGE

1 head cabbage, either green or red, shredded
2 tbsp. butter or margarine
4 tbsp. vinegar
½ cup water
2 tbsp. currant jelly
1 tsp. salt
3 tbsp. sugar

Melt butter or margarine in saucepan. Add cabbage, vinegar, and water. Cover and cook about 30 minutes. Add jelly, salt, and sugar; cook a few more minutes.
Makes 6 servings.

CHINESE CABBAGE

1 bunch chinese cabbage
½ cup water
1 tbsp. soy sauce
1 green pepper, chopped
1 pimento, chopped
1 onion, grated
1 can cream of celery soup (optional)

Slice cabbage crosswise into 1-inch pieces. Wash thoroughly. Drain. Cook quickly in small amount of water (about 10 minutes). Add remaining ingredients; cook about 10 more minutes.
Makes 6 servings.

GLAZED CARROTS

1 lb. whole carrots peeled and cut in 1-inch pieces.
2 cups water
½ cup maple-flavored syrup, or syrup with 1 tsp. maple flavor
3 tbsp. margarine or butter
1 tsp. salt

Cook carrots in salted water until tender, about 30 minutes. Drain. Add syrup and margarine; simmer a few minutes.
Makes 6 servings.

CARROT LOAF

1½ cups ground raw carrots
1 cup cooked rice
1 cup ground peanuts
1 egg
½ tsp. salt

¼ tsp. white pepper
2 tbsp. diced green pepper
1 small onion, diced
½ tsp. dry mustard

Beat egg in bowl; add remaining ingredients. Pour into lightly greased loaf pan. Bake in preheated 350° oven about 45 minutes.
Makes 6 servings.

CARROTS SUPREME

6 carrots, peeled and cut in 1-inch pieces
2 tbsp. butter
1 tsp. salt
¼ tsp. white pepper
1 tbsp. brown sugar
1 cup hot water or dissolve 1 chicken bouillon cube in the water

⅔ cup cream or sour cream
1 egg yolk
1 tbsp. lemon juice
½ cup walnut meats

Cook carrots in broth or water until tender, about 30 minutes. Blend all other ingredients together; fold into carrots. Cook (do not boil) until heated through.
Makes 6 servings.

CAULIFLOWER WITH CHEESE

Immerse whole head of cauliflower, core up, in boiling water to which 1 tsp. salt has been added. Cook about 10 minutes. Remove to serving dish. Pour Cheese Sauce (*see* Index) over cauliflower.

Makes 6 servings.

Note: If desired, break into flowerets, and cook the same way.

CELERY, CREOLE STYLE

1 bunch celery
4 cups water

1 recipe Creole Sauce (*see* Index)

Wash celery; cut crosswise in ¾-inch pieces. Use good leaves, if desired. Cook, covered, about 20 minutes; drain. Combine with Creole Sauce; simmer together about 5 minutes.

Makes 6 servings.

CELERY AND TOMATOES

1 bunch celery
1 can (1 lb. 12 oz.) tomatoes

1 tsp. salt
½ cup water

Drain juice from tomatoes and pour in saucepan. Set tomatoes aside. Save good pieces of celery for relish plate. Chop the good leaves and end pieces to make 2 or 3 cups. Add salted water to tomato liquid and cook celery, covered, about 20 minutes. Add tomatoes; simmer 5 more minutes. Serve.

Makes 6 servings.

Note: One cup of bread cubes may be added, if desired.

CHINESE VEGETABLES

2 cans (1 lb. each) fancy Chinese vegetables, rinsed and drained
1 can (10¾ oz.) cream of mushroom soup
1 can (10¾ oz.) cream of celery soup
1 pkg. (1⅜ oz.) brown gravy mix
1 cup hot water

Mix gravy mix with hot water in saucepan. Add other ingredients and mix well. Heat and serve.

Makes 8 servings

Note: Leftover roast beef, pork, or chicken may be added for a one-dish entree.

SCALLOPED CORN I

1 can (1 lb.) corn (either cream-style or whole kernel)
1 cup milk
2 tbsp. butter or margarine
2 tbsp. flour
1 tsp. salt
dash white pepper
2 eggs, beaten
¼ cup yellow cornmeal

Beat eggs, then add all other ingredients, mixing well. Pour into greased casserole. Bake in preheated oven at 350° about 45 minutes.

Makes 6 servings.

SCALLOPED CORN II

1 can (1 lb.) corn (either cream-style or whole kernel)
1 box prepared corn muffin mix
1 egg

Mix together in bowl. Pour into greased casserole. Bake in accordance with instructions on box.

Makes 6 servings.

CORN AND TOMATO PUDDING

1 can (1 lb.) whole kernel corn
1 can (1 lb.) tomatoes
1 cup bread cubes
2 eggs, beaten
1 tbsp. sugar
1 tbsp. chopped parsley
1 small green pepper, chopped
2 tbsp. butter or margarine, melted
1 tsp. salt
¼ tsp. white pepper

Combine ingredients; place in casserole. Top with bread cubes. Bake in preheated 350° oven about 1 hour. Makes 8 servings.

CREAMED CUCUMBERS

3 cucumbers, peeled and diced
1½ cups White Sauce (*see* Index)
2 tbsp. pimento or minced green pepper

Add cucumbers to mixture as milk of *White Sauce* is added. Then mix in pimento or pepper. Serve when sauce is thickened. Makes 6 servings.

EGGPLANT CASSEROLE

1 medium eggplant
4 cups water
1 tsp. salt
6 slices bacon, fried, drained and crumbled
¼ cup diced onion
1 can (10¾ oz.) tomato soup
1 can (11 oz.) cheddar cheese soup
½ cup buttered crumbs or bran flakes

Peel eggplant; dice into ½-inch cubes. Cook in boiling water to which salt has been added for 5 minutes. Let cool 5 minutes, drain. Set aside. Combine all other ingredients, except crumbs, in greased casserole. Add eggplant; top with crumbs; bake in preheated 375° oven for 30 minutes.
Makes 6 servings.

CHINESE EGGPLANT

1 eggplant	1 tsp. salt
¼ cup cooking oil	1 tbsp. soy sauce
½ lb. lean cooked pork or ham, chopped	½ cup hot water
	1 tbsp. cornstarch
4 stalks celery, diced	⅓ cup cold water
1 large onion, chopped	1 can (1 lb.) mixed Chinese vegetables, drained and rinsed
1 green pepper, diced	
3 green onions, cut in ½-inch pieces, to where green begins	
	1 cup bran flakes (optional)

Peel eggplant; cut into ½-inch cubes. Soak in slightly salted water for 30 minutes; drain.

Place cooking oil in skillet; add pork, next four ingredients, and eggplant. Brown slightly. Turn into casserole. Mix cornstarch with cold water; pour over top. Add salt, soy sauce, and hot water. Spread Chinese vegetables over top. Spread bran flakes over Chinese vegetables. Bake in preheated 350° oven for 45 minutes. Serve immediately.

Makes 6 servings.

EGGPLANT CREOLE

1 medium eggplant
1 recipe Creole Sauce (*see* Index)

Peel and dice eggplant into ½-inch cubes; soak in slightly salted water for 1 hour; drain.

Place eggplant in Creole Sauce while sauce is cooking. Cook for 30 minutes.

Makes 6 servings

FRIED EGGPLANT

1 eggplant	½ tsp. salt
3 eggs, beaten	½ tsp. white pepper
2 cups flour	½ cup cooking oil

Peel and slice eggplant into ¼-inch slices. Soak in slightly salted water for 1 hour. Drain on towels. Mix flour, salt, and pepper. Beat eggs. Dip eggplant slices in beaten egg, then in flour mixture. Fry until golden brown on each side.
Makes 6 servings.

EGGPLANT PARMESAN

1 medium eggplant	2 tsp. oregano
3 eggs	½ lb. mozzarella cheese, sliced
1 cup flour or bread crumbs	1 can (16 oz.) tomato sauce
½ cup cooking oil	with cheese
½ cup grated Parmesan cheese	

Peel and slice eggplant into ¼-inch slices Soak in slightly salted water for 1 hour. Drain. Beat eggs, dip eggplant in eggs, then in flour or crumbs; brown quickly in hot fat.

Layer in casserole, sprinkling Parmesan cheese, oregano, mozzarella cheese, and sauce between the layers. Top with remaining mozzarella cheese. Bake in preheated 350° oven for 1 hour.
Makes 6 servings.

SCALLOPED EGGPLANT

1 eggplant	1 tsp. salt
1 medium onion, diced	½ tsp. white pepper
½ cup milk	½ cup grated cheese
2 eggs, beaten	1 cup bran flakes (optional)
2 tbsp. butter	

Peel eggplant; cut into ½-inch cubes. Soak in slightly salted water for 1 hour; drain.

Layer eggplant and onion in greased casserole. Add milk, eggs, and seasonings; top with grated cheese and bran flakes. Bake in preheated 350° oven for 1 hour.

Makes 6 servings.

EGGPLANT STROGANOFF

1 eggplant, peeled and sliced
1 tbsp. lemon juice
½ tsp. salt
2 onions, sliced thin
3 tomatoes, peeled and sliced

2 tbsp. flour
¼ tsp. salt
¼ tsp. white pepper
1 cup sour cream

Cook eggplant in salted water with lemon juice, about 5 minutes. Drain.

Alternate layers of eggplant, onion, and tomato in casserole. Sprinkle flour, salt, and pepper over top. Spoon sour cream over top. Bake in preheated 350° oven about 45 minutes.

Makes 6 servings.

CREAMED VEGETABLE CASSEROLE

1 medium eggplant or 2 small zucchini
1 can or jar (1 lb.) small whole onions drained
1 can (10¾ oz.) cream of celery soup
1 can (1 lb.) tomatoes

2 tbsp. flour
1 cup sliced celery
1 cup grated cheese
1 tsp. salt
1 tsp. white pepper
2 tbsp. butter or margarine
1 cup bran flakes

If eggplant is used, peel and dice into ½-inch cubes; soak in slightly salted water for 1 hour; drain. If zucchini is used, wash and slice in ½-inch slices. Combine vegetables, half of the cheese, seasonings, and flour. Pour into greased casserole. Top with butter or margarine, the other half of the cheese, and bran flakes. Bake in preheated 350° oven 45 minutes to 1 hour.

Makes 6 servings.

FRIED MUSHROOMS

12 large spring sponge mushrooms (morels)
2 eggs, well beaten

1 cup cracker meal
¼ lb. butter or margarine

Clean mushrooms; cut in half lengthwise. Drain on paper towels. Heat shortening in heavy skillet. Dip mushrooms in egg, then in cracker meal; fry in hot fat slowly until golden brown. Makes 6 servings.

OKRA, RICE, AND TOMATOES

1 qt. okra, washed and sliced
1 cup rice
1 can (1 lb.) tomatoes; reserve liquid
water to measure

2 tbsp. butter
1 tsp. salt
½ tsp. white pepper
¼ tsp. paprika

Wash rice. Drain liquid from tomatoes and add enough water to make 3 cups liquid. Add rice and cook about 15 minutes. Add okra; cook 10 minutes. Add tomatoes and seasonings; simmer 5 minutes longer.
Makes 8 servings.

BAKED ONIONS

2 cans or jars (1 lb. each) small whole cooked onions, drained
¼ cup sugar
1 tsp. prepared mustard

4 tbsp. butter or margarine, softened
¼ tsp. paprika
½ cup bran flakes

Place onions in 8-by-12 baking dish. Mix sugar, mustard, butter or margarine; spread over onions. Top with paprika and bran flakes. Bake in preheated 350° oven for 20 minutes.
Makes 6 servings.

BOILED ONIONS IN WHITE SAUCE

18 medium white onions
1 tsp. salt
4 cups hot water
⅛ lb. butter or margarine, melted
½ cup flour

½ tsp. white pepper
½ tsp. seasoned salt
paprika
1½ cups dry powdered milk

Peel onion, leaving some of the root structure at the bottom of each onion; this holds them together at the bottom. Pierce each onion with a two pronged kitchen fork to keep the tops from popping out. Put onions, salt, and hot water in saucepan. Cook uncovered about 20 minutes.

Blend flour and seasonings with melted butter; mix with dry milk. Add to onions; simmer until thickened. Spoon onions out of sauce, place in serving dish, pour remaining sauce over onions, and sprinkle with more paprika, if desired.

Makes 9 servings.

ONION DELIGHT

3 cans or jars (1 lb. each) small whole cooked onions, drained
1 can (10¾ oz.) cream of mushroom soup

1 can (10¾ oz.) cheddar cheese soup

Place onions in greased casserole or baking pan. Pour soups over onions. Bake in preheated 350° oven for 30 minutes.

Makes 12 servings.

FRIED ONIONS

Peel onion and slice. Insert rounded toothpick from outside edge to at least center of onion slice. Fry in meat drippings or cooking oil until browned on one side; flip over and brown second side. Remove toothpick before serving.

FRENCH-FRIED ONION RINGS

2 large onions
1 egg
½ cup prepared biscuit mix
½ cup buttermilk pancake mix
⅓ cup milk
cracker meal or prepared breading mix
shortening

Peel and slice onions into about ⅛-inch slices. Separate rings. Freeze centers and broken slices for later use.

Beat egg; add dry ingredients and milk. Mix very well. This should be a medium batter.

Dip onion in batter, then in breading. Handle carefully; be sure the entire ring is breaded. Lay on wax paper. The wax paper may be layered, but be sure rings are not touching. Refrigerate at least an hour or overnight before cooking.

Fry in hot shortening until golden brown.
Makes 4 servings.

GLAZED ONIONS

18 medium onions
8 cups boiling water
2 tsp. salt
4 tbsp. butter or margarine, melted
3 tbsp. sugar

Peel onion, leaving some of the root structure at the end of each onion. Cook, uncovered in boiling water for 20 minutes. Use 1½ tsp. of the salt in the water. Drain; put in baking dish. Mix butter or margarine with remaining ½ tsp. salt and sugar. Pour over onions. Bake, uncovered, in preheated 350° oven for ½ hour. Baste frequently with butter mixture while cooking.
Makes 9 servings.

ONION-POTATOES

3 potatoes, peeled and sliced
3 onions, peeled and sliced
3 tbsp. butter or margarine
1 tsp. salt

½ tsp. white pepper
paprika
½ cup bread crumbs

Use covered casserole dish. In greased casserole, layer potatoes and onion alternately. Dot each layer with butter, seasoning, and crumbs. Sprinkle top with paprika. Cover. Bake in preheated 350° oven about 45 minutes. Uncover and brown for 15 minutes.
Makes 6 servings.

PARSNIP FRITTERS

1 lb. parsnips
2 tbsp. butter or margarine
1 tsp. salt

½ tsp. white pepper
1 cup flour
cooking oil

Wash parsnips; cook in boiling water for 15 minutes. Peel parsnips and mash, adding butter or margarine, and salt and pepper. Dip hands into cold water; shape mixture into patties. Dip patties in flour; fry in cooking oil until brown on both sides.
Makes 24 fritters.

SAUTÉED PARSNIPS

1 lb. parsnips (or 2 per serving)
cooking oil

Wash parsnips; cook in boiling water for 10 minutes. Peel. Cut in half lengthwise, then cut stick in half crosswise. Fry in skillet until browned. Salt to taste while frying.

SCALLOPED PARSNIPS

1 lb. parsnips
½ cup cream
2 tbsp. butter or margarine
1 tsp. salt
½ tsp. white pepper
⅛ cup bran flakes or bread crumbs

Wash parsnips; cook in boiling water for 15 minutes; peel. Mash parsnips, adding all ingredients except topping crumbs. Place in casserole dish, top with crumbs. Brown in preheated 350° oven about 20 minutes.
Makes 6 servings.

STUFFED GREEN PEPPERS

4 or 6 large green peppers
1 tbsp. chopped onion
2 tbsp. chopped celery
2 tbsp. cooking oil
2 tsp. flour
½ cup milk
1 cup whole kernel corn
1 cup chopped cooked ham
¼ cup bread crumbs
1 tbsp. margarine or butter

Cut a slice across the top of green pepper. Remove seeds and membrane. Wrap tops and place in freezer to use when grated pepper is desired.

Melt oil; fry onion and celery for two minutes. Blend in flour; add milk; cook over medium heat until thickened. Fold in corn and ham.

Fill pepper with mixture; top with buttered crumbs and margarine. Bake in greased baking dish in preheated 350° oven about 30 minutes.
Makes 4-6 servings.

TWICE-BAKED POTATOES

8 medium Idaho potatoes
3 eggs
½ cup sour cream
⅛ lb. butter or margarine
1 tsp. salt
½ tsp. white pepper

OPTIONAL
¼ cup frozen, freeze-dried, or freshly chopped chives or 1 small onion, diced or ½ cup Parmesan cheese or grated cheddar cheese or 1 cup finely diced ham

Bake potatoes in preheated 450° oven about 45 minutes, or until done; or parboil potatoes in hot water for 15 minutes, then bake until done (a lesser amount of time.)

While still hot, cut off top third of potato and scoop out pulp, being careful not to tear the skin. Include pulp from top third of potato, and mash with eggs and next four ingredients. If any of the optional items are used, fold into potatoes after mashing. Stuff potato shells with mixture, and brush with butter or margarine; return to oven and bake until browned.

HOT DEVILED POTATOES

4 cups warm mashed potatoes
½ cup sour cream
2 tsp. prepared mustard
1 tsp. salt
1 tsp. sugar
¼ tsp. white pepper
2 tbsp. minced onion
paprika

Mix all ingredients except paprika. Place in casserole. Sprinkle with paprika. Bake in preheated oven at 350° for 20 minutes. Makes 6 servings.

MASHED POTATOES

Cook peeled potatoes in boiling salted water until soft. Drain; mash.

To about 4 cups of mashed potatoes add ½ cup milk, 4 tbsp. butter, dash of salt, and white pepper. Beat until fluffy. Save the potato water for the gravy.

An alternate method is to cook potatoes in small quantity of water, mash in the water, and add powdered milk along with butter, salt, and pepper.

INDIVIDUAL MASHED POTATOES

Mash ½ cup potatoes for each serving. Scoop up with ice cream dipper; place on greased cookie sheet. Make small indentation at top with bottom of scoop. Place one pat of butter on top. Sprinkle with paprika, and parsley if desired. Bake in preheated 350° oven for 20 minutes.

Note: Leftover mashed potatoes may be used, or servings may be prepared in advance to heat when entree is served.

IDAHO PIZZA

3 cups warm mashed potatoes
1 tsp. salt
2 tbsp. butter or margarine
1 egg beaten

¼ cup Parmesan cheese
¼ lb. sliced mozzarella cheese
¼ cup imitation bacon bits
1 can (6 oz.) pizza sauce

Mix potatoes with salt, butter, and egg. Press into buttered 10-inch pie plate. Top with mozzarella cheese, imitation bacon, and pizza sauce. Bake in preheated 450° oven for 20 minutes.

Makes 6 servings.

Note: Bake in microwave oven for 2 or 3 minutes.

POTATO PUFF

3 cups mashed potatoes, leftover or freshly mashed
2 eggs, separated
1 tsp. salt

½ tsp. white pepper
2 tbsp. minced onion, chopped chives, or parsley (optional)

Beat egg whites until stiff; fold in remaining ingredients. Bake in preheated 375° oven for 20 or 30 minutes.

Makes 6 servings.

Note: This is not as delicate as a soufflé to handle. If hot potatoes are used, bake immediately for 20 minutes. If cold potatoes are used, or if mixture is made in advance with cold potatoes, or if cooking is to be delayed, bake for 30 minutes.

PARSLEYED NEW POTATOES

2 lbs. new potatoes

Wash and scrape potatoes. Cook in boiling water about 20 minutes, until fork tender. Drain. Roll in Parsley Butter for Sea Food or Potatoes (*see* Index).

Makes 6 servings.

Note: As an alternate, add 1 tbsp. chopped parsley to 2 cups White Sauce (*see* Index); serve creamed. Or add cooked fresh or frozen peas to potatoes.

SCALLOPED POTATOES

6 medium potatoes
2 cups hot water
¼ cup flour
1 tsp. salt

1 tsp. white pepper
2 tbsp. butter or margarine
1 cup dry powdered milk
2 tbsp. minced onion

Wash, peel, and slice potatoes. Put potatoes and hot water in saucepan. Cook for 20 minutes. Remove from heat. Mix flour

Vegetables

with dry milk and seasonings. Layer potatoes and dry mixture in greased casserole. Bake in preheated 350° oven about 45 minutes.

Makes 8 servings.

Note: Eight slices of cheese may be layered with potatoes, or 1 cup cooked diced ham, or both.

SCALLOPED POTATOES AND HAM

8 medium potatoes
3 cups hot water
3 cups cooked ham, cubed
8 slices cheese (optional)
1 onion, minced
1½ tsp. salt
1 tsp. white pepper
¼ cup flour

1 can (10¾ oz.) of one of these soups:
  cream of celery
  cream of chicken
  cream of mushroom
1½ cups dry powdered milk
¼ cup butter or margarine

Wash, peel, and slice potatoes. Put potatoes and 2½ cups of the hot water in saucepan. Cook for 30 minutes. Remove from heat. Add onion and the can of soup. Layer potatoes, ham, cheese, dry mixture of flour, and milk, and seasonings in greased casserole. Top with butter or margarine. Bake in preheated 350° oven for 1 hour.

Makes 12 servings.

CREAMED RADISHES

1 lb. radishes
2 tbsp. butter or margarine
1 tbsp. flour
¼ tsp. curry powder

½ tsp. salt
¼ tsp. white pepper
1 cup hot water
¼ cup dry powdered milk

Wash radishes; cut off ends. Halve each radish. Place in saucepan; add water and cook about 15 minutes. Mix flour with dry powdered milk; add it and rest of ingredients to radishes. Cook until thickened.

Makes 6 servings.

HOT SAUERKRAUT

1 can (1 lb. 11 oz.) sauerkraut
1 apple, peeled and sliced
2 tbsp. caraway seed
1 large onion, chopped

1 cup white wine, or ¼ cup vinegar
¼ cup butter or margarine

Combine all ingredients. Heat on top of stove or bake in covered casserole in preheated 350° oven about 45 minutes. Makes 6 servings.

BAKED SQUASH WITH APPLE

4 acorn squash
1 can (1 15. 5 oz.) prepared instant apple pie mix
8 tbsp. butter or margarine, melted

1 cup brown sugar
1 tbsp. lemon juice
½ tsp. pumpkin pie spice
½ tsp. cinnamon

Pierce squash with kitchen fork to allow steam to escape. Immerse whole in large kettle of hot water. Cook for 30 minutes, or place on cookie sheet in 350° preheated oven for 30 minutes.

While squash is cooking, combine other ingredients, except melted butter.

Remove squash from kettle or oven, halve lengthwise, remove seeds, and brush with melted butter; fill centers equally with apple mixture; bake in 350° preheated oven for 30 minutes. Makes 8 servings.

CANADIAN BACON-SQUASH CASSEROLE

6 slices Canadian-style bacon, cut ½ inch thick
2 pkgs. (10 oz. each) frozen cooked squash, thawed; or 2 cups cooked squash, mashed

¼ cup brown sugar
¼ cup sugar
½ tsp. cinnamon
¾ cup fresh cranberries, cut in half
¼ cup chopped walnuts

Vegetables

Combine all ingredients, except bacon; pour in greased casserole. Place bacon on top. Bake in preheated 350° oven about 45 minutes.
Makes 6 servings.

SQUASH WITH BACON

2 pkgs. (10 oz. each) frozen cooked squash, thawed
6 strips bacon
½ tsp. salt
¼ tsp. white pepper
1 tbsp. sugar
3 tbsp. butter or margarine
1 cup milk

Mix all ingredients except bacon. Turn into greased casserole; top with bacon strips. Bake in preheated 350° oven for 20 minutes.
Makes 6 servings.

GLAZED SQUASH

2 acorn squash
¼ cup sugar
¼ cup brown sugar
½ cup orange juice
2 tbsp. butter or margarine

ACORN SQUASH

Precook acorn squash before you cut it. Simply pierce the squash with two-pronged kitchen fork and place in preheated oven for 15 minutes; or parboil in kettle of water for 15 minutes.

Split and scoop out seeds of precooked squash. Heat together sugars, juice, and butter or margarine. Pour syrup mixture over squash. Bake in preheated 375° oven for 30 minutes.
Makes 4 servings.

BAKED HUBBARD SQUASH

Cut Hubbard squash into serving-size pieces. Dot each piece with butter or bacon or ham drippings. Sprinkle with salt and white pepper. Bake in preheated 400° oven about 45 minutes. May also be sprinkled with brown sugar.

Note: Squash may be parboiled 5 or 10 minutes to shorten cooking time, and make it easier to cut.

SQUASH MANDARIN

2 lbs. yellow summer squash
1 tsp. salt
2 tbsp. butter or margarine
1 can (11 oz.) mandarin oranges
2 tbsp. brown sugar
¼ tsp. nutmeg
¼ cup slivered almonds

Wash squash; cut crosswise in ½-inch slices. Cook until just tender. Drain; butter; keep hot. Set aside. Pour syrup from oranges into saucepan; add sugar and boil a few minutes. Add oranges, nuts, sugar, and nutmeg. Pour mixture over squash. Serve.

Makes 6 servings.

CANDIED SWEET POTATOES

6 large sweet potatoes
1 tsp. salt
½ tsp. white pepper
⅛ lb. butter or margarine
1 cup brown sugar
¼ cup maple syrup (optional)
½ cup water
1 tsp. cinnamon
¼ tsp. nutmeg
½ tsp. pumpkin or apple pie spice

Cook sweet potatoes in skins; peel and quarter. Place in greased baking pan. (Potatoes may be brushed with lemon juice

Vegetables

to keep from discoloring.) Sprinkle remaining ingredients over potatoes. Bake in preheated 350° oven for 20 minutes.
Makes 8 servings.

SWEET POTATO CASSEROLE

4 sweet potatoes, cooked, peeled and sliced ½-inch thick
1 orange, unpeeled, sliced and halved
½ cup apple or currant jelly
2 tbsp. margarine
1 tsp. cinnamon
½ tsp. nutmeg
½ tsp. salt
1 cup white miniature marshmallows

Arrange sweet potatoes and orange slices in casserole. Sprinkle jelly, margarine, and seasonings over top. Bake in preheated 350° oven about 20 minutes. Spread marshmallows over top, return to oven, and bake until marshmallows are melted and lightly browned.
Makes 6 servings.

CREOLE SWEET POTATOES

6 large yams, cooked and peeled
⅛ lb. butter
¼ tsp. vanilla or maple flavoring
1 tsp. cinnamon
⅛ tsp. ground cloves
⅛ tsp. nutmeg
½ cup brown sugar
1 tsp. salt
½ cup white seedless raisins
1 cup white miniature marshmallows

Mash sweet potatoes; mix with all ingredients, except marshmallows. Transfer potatoes to a greased baking pan. Bake in preheated 375° oven for 20 minutes. Spread marshmallows over top; bake until marshmallows are melted and lightly browned.
Makes 8 servings.

SWEET POTATO PIE

2 cups cooked and mashed sweet potatoes	1/8 tsp. nutmeg
1 cup milk	1/8 tsp. pumpkin or apple pie spice
2 eggs, beaten	1/4 tsp. vanilla or maple flavoring
1 tbsp. butter or margarine	1/4 tsp. salt
1/3 cup brown sugar	1 tbsp. flour
1 tbsp. molasses	1 cup white miniature marshmallows
1/2 tsp. cinnamon	1 unbaked pie shell (optional)
1/8 tsp. ground ginger	

To the mashed sweet potatoes add all other ingredients, except marshmallows. Mix very well. Place in unbaked pie shell or greased round casserole. Bake in preheated 425° oven 30 to 40 minutes. Top with marshmallows; bake until they melt and brown slightly. Serve, hot, cold, or warm.
Makes 6 servings.

SWEET POTATO PUFF

3 cups cooked and mashed sweet potatoes	2 eggs, beaten
1 can (6 oz.) undiluted evaporated milk	1 tsp. salt
1/4 cup margarine, melted	1 cup white miniature marshmallows
1/3 cup brown sugar	1/2 cup chopped walnuts

Combine all ingredients, except marshmallows. Mix well. Pour into greased casserole. Bake in preheated 350° oven for 30 minutes. Top with marshmallows; return to oven until marshmallows are melted and lightly browned.
Makes 4 servings.

Vegetables

YAMS AND PINEAPPLE

4 large yams, cooked and peeled
8 pineapple rings
½ cup brown sugar
2 tbsp. butter

½ tsp. salt
½ tsp. cinnamon
½ tsp. nutmeg

Slice sweet potatoes lengthwise. Cut ¼ inch off rounded end. Place cut side down on greased baking pan. Top with pineapple slice. Mash the 8 pieces of potato that were cut off, and place in center of pineapple ring (heap on top). Dot top of each half of potato with butter, salt, cinnamon and nutmeg. Bake in preheated 375° oven about 15 minutes.

Makes 8 servings.

SUCCOTASH

2 cups lima beans, fresh, canned, or frozen (preferably green limas)
2 cups corn, fresh, canned, or frozen (preferably whole kernel)

⅔ cup milk or cream
3 tbsp. butter or margarine

Cook beans and corn separately until done, if fresh or frozen are used. If canned beans and corn are used, combine in pan, bring to boiling point.

Add milk and butter. Heat.

Makes 6 servings.

FRIED GREEN TOMATOES

12 green tomatoes
1 tsp. salt
2 eggs, beaten

1 cup flour
½ cup cooking oil

Slice tomatoes about ¼ inch thick. Place in bowl; cover with salted water and let stand for 15 minutes. Remove tomatoes from water and drain on towel. Handle slices carefully. Dip in beaten egg, then in flour; fry in hot oil until brown on both sides. Makes 8 servings.

STEWED TOMATOES

8 fresh tomatoes or 1 can (1 lb. 12 oz.) tomatoes
2 tbsp. butter

1 tsp. salt
¼ tsp. white pepper
4 slices hard bread or toast

If fresh tomatoes are used, pour boiling water over them and let stand a few minutes; drain and peel. Cut in quarters. If canned tomatoes are used, cut in quarters.

If fresh tomatoes are used, add 1 cup water to saucepan and cook until tender, about 15 minutes. If canned tomatoes are used, pour tomatoes and juice in saucepan and heat.

When hot add butter and seasonings, stir until butter melts, pour into serving dish, and top with dry bread and serve. Makes 6 servings.

MASHED TURNIPS

1 lb. turnips, peeled and cooked
4 tbsp. butter or margarine
½ tsp. salt

¼ tsp. white pepper
⅓ cup powdered milk, dry

Mash turnips; add other ingredients. Mix well. Serve. Makes 6 servings.

SEVEN-LAYER VEGETABLE CASSEROLE

1 cup uncooked rice
1 can (1 lb.) whole kernel corn
2 cans (8 oz.) tomato sauce, plus 1 can water
1 onion, chopped
1 green pepper, chopped
1 zucchini or eggplant
1 cup chopped celery
1 tsp. salt
½ tsp. white pepper
6 strips bacon, cut in half

If using eggplant, peel, cube, and soak in hot water with 1 tsp. salt while preparing other vegetable. If using zucchini, cut and cube. Do not peel.

Add rice to casserole; layer other vegetables; top with tomato sauce, salt, and pepper. Lay strips of bacon, uncooked, over top. Cover; bake in 350° preheated oven for 1 hour. Uncover and bake for 30 minutes longer.

Makes 8 servings.

ZUCCHINI CASSEROLE

2 small zucchini
1 medium onion, chopped
6 tbsp. butter
1 cup shredded cheese
1 tsp. salt
½ tsp. white pepper
2 eggs
1½ cup soft bread crumbs or bran flakes

Do not peel the zucchini; cut into ¼-inch slices. Beat eggs in mixing bowl. Add all ingredients, except crumbs. Place in greased casserole, top with crumbs. Bake in 350° oven 1 hour.

Makes 6 servings.

ZUCCHINI CREOLE

2 small zucchini
1 recipe Creole Sauce (*see* Index)

Wash and slice (unpeeled) zucchini into ½-inch slices. Place zucchini in Creole Sauce while sauce is cooking. Cook for 30 minutes.
Makes 6 servings.

ZUCCHINI-EGGPLANT CASSEROLE

1 zucchini
1 eggplant
3 onions, sliced thin
1 green pepper, cut in strips

1 cup cooking oil
5 oz. stuffed green olives
1 tbsp. seasoned salt
¼ tsp. white pepper

Cut zucchini into ½-inch slices; do not peel. Peel eggplant and cut in ½-inch slices; soak in slightly salted water for 1 hour; drain.

Sauté green pepper and onion in oil a few minutes. Add all other ingredients. Cover; cook for 20 minutes. Pour ingredients into greased casserole. Place in preheated 400° oven. Bake another 20 minutes.
Makes 12 servings.

ITALIAN-STYLE ZUCCHINI

2 (1 lb. size) zucchini, sliced ¼ inch thick
2 stalks celery, sliced ¼ inch thick
1 can (8 oz.) tomato sauce with cheese
¼ tsp. salt

¼ tsp. white pepper
2 tbsp. melted butter or margarine
dash garlic powder
dash thyme
dash basil

Combine ingredients in heavy saucepan; cook until vegetables are barely tender; or bake in casserole in 375° preheated oven about 30 minutes.
Makes 6 servings.

ZUCCHINI PARMESAN

2 small zucchini
3 eggs
1 cup flour or bread crumbs
½ cup cooking oil
½ cup grated Parmesan cheese
2 tsp. oregano
½ lb. mozzarella cheese, sliced
1 can (16 oz.) tomato sauce with cheese

Wash and slice zucchini (unpeeled) into ½-inch slices. Beat eggs; dip zucchini in eggs, then in flour or crumbs; brown quickly in hot fat.

Layer in casserole, sprinkling Parmesan cheese, oregano, mozzarella cheese, and sauce between the layers. Top with remaining mozzarella cheese. Bake in preheated 350° oven for 1 hour.
Makes 6 servings.

STUFFED ZUCCHINI

3 zucchini
1 small onion, chopped
¼ cup butter or margarine
1 cup rice
2 cups water
¼ cup chopped parsley
1 cup sour cream
½ tsp. salt
¼ tsp. white pepper

Add 2 cups water to rice; put on stove to cook until water is absorbed while preparing rest of ingredients.

Cut zucchini in half lengthwise. Parboil in salted water for 10 minutes. Drain. Carefully scoop out the pulp and chop. Sauté onion in shortening until slightly browned; mix with zucchini pulp, parsley, and sour cream. Add cooked rice to mixture; add seasonings. Spoon into zucchini shells. Place on greased baking pan, and bake in preheated 375° oven about 20 minutes.
Makes 6 servings.

7

RICE AND PASTA

FRIED RICE

3 cups cooked rice
3 tbsp. flour
¼ cup milk

2 tbsp. butter or margarine
1 small minced onion

Combine rice, flour, and milk. Heat butter or margarine in skillet; sauté onions a few minutes. Spread the rice mixture evenly in the skillet; cook over medium heat until golden brown. Turn, as in turning a pancake, brown other side. Serve.
Makes 4 servings.

RICE AU GRATIN

3 cups cooked rice, hot
¾ cup cheddar cheese, grated
3 tbsp. butter or margarine

½ tsp. curry powder
1 slice toast, cut in small cubes

Layer rice and cheese in greased baking dish. Sprinkle remaining ingredients over top. Bake in preheated oven at 350° about 15 minutes.
Makes 4 servings.

RICE O'BRIEN

1 cup rice
2 cups water
3 chicken bouillon cubes
1 tsp. salt
¼ cup butter or margarine
½ cup green onions, sliced from root end to beginning of the green

1 small green pepper, diced
3 tbsp. pimento, diced (optional)
½ cup pitted ripe olives, sliced

Sauté rice, green onion, and green pepper in skillet until lightly browned. Add remaining ingredients. Cover; cook until rice is tender.
Makes 4 servings.

PARSLEY RICE

1 cup rice
1 tsp. salt
2 chicken bouillon cubes
2 cups water
½ cup green onion, sliced from root end to green

⅛ cup green pepper, diced
¼ cup slivered almonds
2 tbsp. margarine
½ cup parsley, chopped

Sauté green onion and pepper in margarine a few minutes. Add remaining ingredients. Cover. Cook until rice is tender.
Makes 4 servings.

SAFFRON RICE RING

1½ cups rice
3 cups chicken broth
⅛ tsp. saffron, crumbled

2½ tsp. butter or margarine
¼ tsp. salt

Combine ingredients in heavy saucepan with cover. Cover; cook over low heat about 20 minutes. Spoon into greased ring mold; pack lightly. Let stand a few minutes. Unmold on heated serving platter.
Makes 6 servings.

CRAB PILAF

2 cans (7½ oz. each) crab meat, drained
3 tbsp. butter or margarine
1 onion, chopped
½ cup celery, chopped
1 pkg. (6 oz.) white and wild rice with seasoning
2 cups hot water
1 apple, peeled and diced
2 tbsp. raisins
2 tsp. curry powder
1 tsp. salt
1 tbsp. chopped parsley

In skillet with cover, sauté onion and celery in butter or margarine until tender. Stir in remaining ingredients. Bring to a boil. Lower heat, cover skillet, simmer 25 minutes, stirring once or twice.
Makes 6 servings.

TUNA PILAF

2 cans (6½-7 oz. each) tuna
2 tbsp. minced onion
2 stalks celery, cut in ¼-inch slices
¼ lb. fresh mushrooms or 1 can (3 oz.) sliced mushrooms or 1 can (10¾ oz.) cream of mushroom soup
3 cups hot water if using fresh or canned mushrooms; reduce to 2½ cups if using the soup
1 green pepper, cut in ¼-inch strips
1 pimento, cut in strips; if not in season, use 2 green peppers or ¼ cup canned pimento
1½ cups rice
2 tbsp. butter or margarine
1 tsp. salt
½ tsp. white pepper
¼ tsp. thyme
2 tsp. Worcestershire sauce

Drain oil from tuna into skillet; add onion, celery, mushrooms (if fresh are used); sauté a few minutes. Add remaining ingredients (except tuna); cover and cook 30 minutes. Add tuna, cook 5 more minutes.
Makes 6 servings.

SOUTHERN PUDDING
(A Complement for Baked Ham)

2 cups rice, cooked
2 eggs
1 cup cheddar cheese, grated
1 can (1 lb.) cream-style golden corn
1 small onion, minced
1 small green pepper, chopped
½ tsp. salt
⅛ tsp. white pepper

Beat eggs; stir in remaining ingredients. Pour into greased casserole. Bake in preheated 350° oven about 1 hour.
Makes 6 servings.

SUNSHINE RICE

1 cup rice
4 tbsp. butter or margarine
1 can (8½ oz.) pineapple tidbits; reserve liquid
2 cups liquid; use juice from pineapple and add enough water to measure

Place in covered saucepan; cook until tender. Serve with pork or chicken entree.
Makes 4 servings.

QUICK-SOAK METHOD OF PREPARING WILD RICE

Wash required amount of wild rice under cold water. Add 3 times amount of boiling water. Parboil for 5 minutes, covered. Remove from heat; let soak in cooking water for 1 hour. Drain; rinse; cook as directed in recipe.

WILD RICE CASSEROLE

1 cup wild rice
1 beef or chicken bouillon cube
3 cups very hot water
¼ cup butter or margarine
½ cup chopped onion

½ cup chopped celery
1 can (3 oz.) sliced, broiled-in-butter mushrooms
½ tsp. salt

Follow the Quick-Soak Method for preparing rice; then sauté onion and celery in margarine or butter for a few minutes in a heavy saucepan with cover. Add remaining ingredients; simmer on top of stove for about 1 hour. Place in greased casserole; bake in preheated 350° oven for 30 minutes.
Makes 4 servings.

FETTUCCINI WITH CHIVES

1 pkg. (12 oz.) noodles; dry, frozen, or homemade
8 cups water
⅛ lb. butter or margarine
1 onion, diced
¼ cup Parmesan cheese, grated
2 tbsp. chopped chives; frozen, fresh, or freeze-dried

8 slices American cheese
1 can (11 oz.) cheddar cheese soup
1 tsp. salt
¼ tsp. white pepper
2 drops yellow food coloring (optional)
2 cups powdered milk

Cook noodles in water until about half done. Add all the other ingredients; simmer about 30 minutes.
Makes 12 servings.

MACARONI AND CHEESE

1 pkg. (8 oz.) macaroni
7 cups water
8 slices cheese, cheddar or American
1 can (11 oz.) cheddar cheese soup

4 tbsp. butter or margarine
2 drops yellow food coloring (optional)
1 tsp. salt
¼ tsp. white pepper
3 cups powdered milk

Combine all ingredients in heavy saucepan. Watch carefully and bring to a boil. Turn heat down; cook 15 minutes. Serve immediately or place in a casserole in oven; sprinkle with paprika, and brown.

Makes 6-8 servings.

MACARONI CREOLE

1 pkg. (8 oz.) macaroni	1 tsp. salt
4 cups tomato juice	1 can (6 oz.) tomato paste, plus
2 cups hot water	1 can water
¼ lb. margarine or butter	1 tsp. seasoned salt
1 green pepper, chopped	1 tsp. chili powder
1 (1 lb. 8 oz.) tomatoes	1 tbsp. sugar
1 onion, minced	1 bay leaf
1 can (6 oz.) mushrooms, stems & pieces	1 tsp. white pepper

Combine all ingredients in a large saucepan. Cook over medium heat about 30 minutes. Remove bay leaf before serving.

Makes 8 servings.

Part 2
THE COLD BUFFET

8

HEARTY SALADS

CORNED BEEF SALAD

1 cup cooked corned beef, cut into ¼-inch cubes
½ cup finely chopped celery
2 tbsp. minced onion
½ cup mayonnaise
2 tbsp. prepared mustard

Combine ingredients. Chill. Makes 4 servings.
Note: Serve on lettuce cups as a salad, or as a spread for sandwiches.

PICKLED BOLOGNA

1 ring (1 lb.) coarse ground bologna
1 onion, sliced
½ cup sugar
½ cup water
1 cup sweet cider vinegar

Skin bologna; cut into slices. Layer in jar with onion. Pour other ingredients in jar; shake. Let stand 24 hours in refrigerator.

CHERRY CHICKEN MOLD

Ring Mold
1 can (1 lb.) pitted bing cherries; reserve liquid
1 pkg. (6 oz.) bing cherry gelatin

2 cups very hot water
¼ cup lemon juice
1 can (12 oz.) ginger ale

Chicken Salad
2½-3 cups cooked chicken, diced
⅔ cup diced celery
¼ cup diced green pepper
⅓ cup slivered almonds

⅔ cup mayonnaise or salad dressing
½ tsp. salt
⅛ tsp. white pepper
1 tsp. soy sauce

To prepare *ring mold:* Drain cherries; measure liquid and add cold water if necessary to make 1 cup. Dissolve gelatin in 2 cups very hot water and pour into 1½-quart mold. Add cherry juice and lemon juice. Stir ginger ale into gelatin mixture, pouring slowly. Chill until partially set, then fold in cherries. Chill until firm.

To prepare *chicken salad:* Combine ingredients. Chill for at least an hour.

Unmold cherry ring; serve with chicken salad in center. Makes 8 servings.

PARTY MOLD

1 cup cooked chicken, diced
1 pkg. (3 oz.) lemon gelatin
1 cup very hot water
½ cup cold water

½ cup mayonnaise or salad dressing
½ cup chopped celery
1 avocado, peeled and diced

Dissolve gelatin in hot water, then add cold water; place in 4-cup ring mold in refrigerator and chill 10 minutes. Stir in mayonnaise or salad dressing. Chill until set.

Unmold on salad greens; fill center with chicken, celery, and avocado. Serve with favorite dressing.

Makes 4 servings.

CHICKEN DIET PLATE

2 slices breast of chicken
½ cup cottage cheese
1 tsp. diced green pepper
½ tsp. minced onion

dash salt
dash white pepper
1 tbsp. low-calorie salad dressing

For each serving, mix together cottage cheese, green pepper, onion, seasoning, and salad dressing. Top with chicken slices. Garnish with tomato wedge if desired.

QUICK-MOLDED CRAB SALAD

1 can (7½ oz.) crab meat, drained and flaked
1 pkg. (3 oz.) lemon gelatin
¾ cup very hot water
4 medium ice cubes
¼ tsp. salt
dash white pepper

4 tbsp. lemon juice
⅓ cup mayonnaise or salad dressing
⅓ cup celery, chopped
2 stuffed green olives, sliced
2 tbsp. green pepper, minced

Combine gelatin and hot water; mix; add ice cubes, stirring until they melt. Add salt, pepper, lemon juice, and mayonnaise; beat until smooth. Pour in 4-cup mold and place in freezer compartment until congealed but still soft.

Add remaining ingredients; chill in refrigerator or freezer until firm. Do not freeze.

Makes 6 servings.

DEVILED EGG SALAD

6 hard cooked eggs, peeled
½ tsp. prepared horseradish
¼ tsp. dry mustard
½ tsp. Worcestershire sauce

½ cup mayonnaise or salad dressing
1 tsp. cut chives or grated onion
2 tbsp. sweet pickle relish

Mash the egg yolks; chop the whites. Add all ingredients to bowl. Mix to smooth consistency. Chill.

Makes 4 servings.

GEN'S FAMOUS EGG SALAD

16 hard-boiled eggs, diced or grated
1 pkg. (1¼ oz.) prepared onion soup mix
1¼ oz. imitation bacon

1¼ cup mayonnaise or salad dressing
2 tbsp. Western-style French dressing

Mix last four ingredients together; set aside to marinate while preparing eggs, then mix all together. Chill. Makes 12 servings.

HAM SALAD

3 cups ham, cooked and cubed
6 hard-cooked eggs, chopped
1 cup celery, diced
½ cup sweet pickle relish or chopped sweet pickle

1 cup mayonnaise or salad dressing
2 tsp. prepared mustard or ½ tsp. dry mustard
dash white pepper

Combine all ingredients; mix well; chill before serving. Makes 8 servings.

HAM SANDWICH SPREAD SALAD

3 cups ham, cooked and ground
½ cup mayonnaise or salad dressing
1 cup pickle relish, drained

1 tsp. horseradish
1 tsp. minced onion
1 tsp. prepared mustard

Combine ingredients. Mix and chill.
Makes 12 sandwiches.

SOUTH AFRICAN GOURMET SALAD

24 oz. South African Rock Lobster Tails, any size	1 tsp. salt
2 lbs. potatoes, cooked and cut into cubes	¼ tsp. white pepper
	1½ cups mayonnaise or salad dressing
1 small onion, diced	¼ cup sour cream

Follow basic directions for boiling lobster according to size selected. When cooked, drench with cold water; drain. Cut away underside membrane; remove meat from shells. Chill. Cut into ¼-inch pieces.

Mix all ingredients except lobster; chill until serving time. At serving time, add lobster and toss together until blended. Makes 8 servings.

JELLIED SALMON SALAD

1 can (1 lb.) salmon, drained and flaked; reserve liquid	1½ cups salmon liquid and cold water to measure
1 pkg. (6 oz.) lemon gelatin	salad greens
2 cups hot water	¼ cup French dressing
1 cup mayonnaise or salad dressing	2 tomatoes cut in wedges (optional)
2 hard-cooked eggs, chopped	1 avocado, sliced (optional)
⅓ cup stuffed olives, chopped	

Dissolve gelatin in 2 cups hot water. Add salmon, mayonnaise, eggs, olives, and liquid, and mix well. Pour into 1½-quart ring mold. Chill until firm. Unmold on salad greens; fill center with French dressing; decorate with tomatoes and avocado. Makes 8 servings.

SALMON SALAD

2 cups salmon, flaked
6 hard-cooked eggs, peeled and chopped
1 cup celery, diced
1½ cups salad dressing or mayonnaise
1 tbsp. lemon juice
½ tsp. horseradish
¼ tsp. salt

Mix all ingredients together. Makes 6 servings.

TUNA SALAD

Substitute tuna for salmon.

TUNA SANDWICH SPREAD SALAD

1 can (7 oz.) tuna, drained and flaked
2 tbsp. minced celery
1 cup sandwich spread

Combine. Makes 8 sandwiches.

TUNA LOAF

1 can (7 oz.) tuna, drained and flaked
1 pkg. (3 oz.) lemon gelatin
2 egg yolks
2 cups milk
1 tsp. salt
¼ tsp. white pepper
¼ tsp. paprika
1 tsp. prepared mustard

In top of double boiler, combine egg yolks and 1½ cups of the milk. Cook, stirring constantly, until mixture thickens. Soften gelatin in remaining milk; add to mixture. Add remaining ingredients. Mix. Pour into 4-cup mold. Chill. Unmold on salad greens.

Makes 6 servings.

TUNA MOUSSE

1 can (9¼ oz.) tuna
1 box (6 oz.) lemon gelatin
2 chicken bouillon cubes
4 cups water, 2 hot, 2 cold
½ cup mayonnaise or salad dressing
1 tsp. minced onion
3 drops Tabasco sauce
½ cup grated cheese
4 tbsp. sweet pickle relish
1 cup salad croutons
½ cup heavy cream, whipped

Soften bouillon cubes and gelatin in hot water. Add cold water and remaining ingredients, except croutons and whipped cream. Mix well before folding in croutons and whipped cream. Pour into 1½-quart mold. Chill.

Makes 8 servings.

TUNA WALDORF SALAD

1 can (7 oz.) tuna
1 red apple
1 tbsp. lemon juice
1 cup cooked peas
1 tbsp. pickle relish
½ cup chopped cooked carrot
⅔ cup mayonnaise

Chop apple in bowl with lemon juice, mixing as you chop. Add and mix remaining ingredients. Chill.

Makes 6 servings.

9

FRUIT, VEGETABLE, AND OTHER MOLDED SALADS

HOLLAND-STYLE APPLE SALAD

1 pkg. (3 oz.) lemon gelatin
2 cups minus 2 tbsp. very hot water
2 tsp. vinegar
¼ tsp. salt
1 large red apple, diced
½ cup diced celery
¼ cup chopped English walnut meats

Dissolve gelatin in very hot water. Add vinegar and salt. Pour into 4-cup mold and chill until slightly thickened. Add apples, celery, and nuts. Chill until firm.
Makes 6 servings.

APPLE SALAD

4 large or 8 medium red, tart, firm apples
1 cup mayonnaise or salad dressing
1 cup heavy cream, whipped, or 1 cup sour cream
1 cup celery, chopped fine
1 can (15¼ oz.) pineapple tidbits, drained
1 can (1 lb.) seedless grapes, drained, or 1 lb. fresh seedless grapes, halved
1 cup powdered sugar
1 tbsp. lemon juice
1 cup miniature marshmallows
½ cup chopped English walnut meats

Mix all ingredients, except apples in mixing bowl. Wash and cut apples in quarters. Remove core. Chop into ¼-inch pieces, adding to salad mixture as each quarter is chopped to prevent discoloration. Stir gently. Chill in refrigerator for about an hour. Makes 16 servings.

SPICY APPLESAUCE MOLD

1 pkg. (3 oz.) apple gelatin
1 cup very hot water
¼ cup red-hots (red cinnamon candies)
1 can (1 lb.) applesauce
1 tbsp. sugar
1 tbsp. lemon juice

Dissolve candy and gelatin in hot water. Pour into 4-cup mold. Add remaining ingredients. Chill.
Makes 6 servings.

APRICOT FIZZ SALAD

1 pkg. (6 oz.) orange gelatin
1 can (15¼ oz.) pineapple tidbits
1 can (1 lb.) apricots, each half chopped in 4 pieces
1 can (11 oz.) mandarin oranges
1 can (12 oz.) sweet soda

Drain juice from fruit; measure and heat, then pour over gelatin in large mixing bowl (use large bowl, because soda fizzes when it is added). Stir until gelatin is dissolved, then add enough cold water to make 2 cups liquid. Add fruit; stir. Add soda. Pour into 2-quart mold. Chill until set.
Makes 12 servings.

Fruit, Vegetable, and Molded Salads

AVOCADO ON THE HALF SHELL

2 avocados
1 orange, peeled and sectioned
1 grapefruit, peeled and sectioned

½ cup diced celery
16 pitted ripe olives, sliced
salad dressing*

Cut ripe avocados in half lengthwise, without peeling. Remove pit. Divide fruit evenly and place into the four avocado shells. Sprinkle celery and olives over top.

*Note: Serve plain or use any of the following: Fruit Salad Dressing (see Index), mayonnaise or salad dressing, or Western-style French dressing.

BANANA SALAD

1 pkg. (5 oz.) banana pudding mix (not instant)
1 can (1 lb.) fruit cocktail or (15¼ oz.) can pineapple tidbits

1 cup dry powdered milk
1 cup miniature marshmallows
2 or 3 bananas, sliced

Drain fruit; measure juice and add enough hot water to make 3 cups. Set aside. Cook pudding mix using water and fruit juice mixture. Add dry milk and stir. Let cool. Add fruit cocktail or pineapple. Add marshmallows. Just before serving, add bananas, pushing down into salad so they will not discolor.

Makes 12 servings.

Note: This salad will keep in refrigerator a week. Bananas may be added as it is served. If using individual sherbet glasses, place sliced bananas in bottom of glass, then put pudding mixture on top.

BANANA-APRICOT SALAD

1 can (1 lb. 5 oz.) prepared instant apricot pie mix
1 can (15¼ oz.) crushed pineapple
1 cup miniature marshmallows
2 or 3 bananas, sliced

Mix pie mix, pineapple, and marshmallows together. Chill. Add bananas just before serving, pushing down into salad so they will not discolor.
Makes 12 servings.

BEAN SPROUT SALAD

2 cans (1 lb. each) bean sprouts, rinsed and drained
1 small onion, finely chopped
2 tbsp. soy sauce
2 tbsp. Western-style French dressing
1 tbsp. vegetable oil
1 tbsp. sugar
½ tsp. seasoned salt
⅛ tsp. white pepper

Combine all ingredients, chill and serve.
Makes 12 servings.
Note: Will keep 10 days in refrigerator.

KIDNEY BEAN SALAD

1 can (1 lb.) kidney beans, rinsed and well-drained
4 hard-cooked eggs, peeled and diced
¼ cup sweet pickle relish, drained
½ cup finely chopped celery
2 tbsp. minced onion
½ tsp. salt
⅛ tsp. white pepper
4 slices American or cheddar cheese, chopped fine
1½ cups mayonnaise or salad dressing
2 tbsp. imitation bacon bits (optional)

Combine ingredients. Chill.
Makes 8 servings.
Note: For pea salad use 1 can (1 lb.) peas or 2 pkgs. (10 oz. each) frozen peas, cooked and drained.

MUSTARD BEANS

2 cans (16 oz. each) yellow wax beans, drained, reserving liquid
1 cup sugar
3 tbsp. prepared yellow mustard
1 small onion, minced
½ tsp. salt
½ tsp. white pepper
¾ cup sweet cider vinegar

Combine liquid from beans with sugar; heat and stir until dissolved. Add beans and remaining ingredients; simmer 5 minutes. Cool. Cover and refrigerate overnight before serving. Will keep for 10 days in the refrigerator.
Makes 12 servings.

THREE-BEAN SALAD

1 can (1 lb.) red kidney beans, drained and rinsed
1 can (1 lb.) cut green beans, drained and rinsed
1 can (1 lb.) yellow wax beans, drained and rinsed
1 cup diced celery
1 small red onion, chopped fine
½ cup pimento, chopped very fine
¾ cup wine vinegar
1 tbsp. vegetable oil
2 tbsp. Western-style French dressing
¼ cup sugar
¼ tsp. nutmeg
¼ tsp. salt
½ tsp. seasoned salt
⅛ tsp. white pepper
1 tsp. Worcestershire sauce

Beans may be drained and rinsed together; shake so that no water remains before adding to salad.

Toss beans together in large bowl. Combine rest of ingredients; pour over beans. Refrigerate several hours before serving.
Makes 18 servings.

FOUR-BEAN SALAD

Add 1 can (1 lb.) green baby lima beans, drained and rinsed, to ingredients for Three-Bean Salad (*see* above).
Makes 24 servings.
Note: Salads will keep in refrigerator for 10 days.

PICKLED BEETS

4 cans (1 lb. each) small whole or sliced beets. Drain, reserving liquid
3 cups vinegar
2 cups beet juice (add enough water to make 2 cups)
2½ cups sugar
2 tsp. salt
1 tbsp. pickling spice

Place beets in container with cover; set aside. Heat all other ingredients together, bringing just to boiling point. Stir once or twice to be sure sugar is dissolved. Pour liquid through tea strainer when pouring over beets. Cool. Store in refrigerator. Will keep in refrigerator indefinitely.

PICKLED EGGS

When beets are gone, place ten hard-boiled and peeled eggs in the remaining liquid. Marinate at least 2 days.

Makes 20 servings.

Note: If beets and eggs are going to be used within 10 days, they may be mixed together; otherwise do not add eggs. A few drops of red food coloring may be added to give eggs a redder color.

BROKEN GLASS SALAD

1 pkg. (3 oz.) lime gelatin
3½ cups very hot water
1 pkg. (3 oz.) raspberry, cherry, or strawberry gelatin
2 cups miniature marshmallows
1 cup crushed pineapple, drained
1 cup heavy cream, whipped

Dissolve gelatin separately, using 1¾ cups water for each flavor. Pour into two separate 8-inch square pans. Chill. Cut into 1-inch square cubes. Fold pineapple and marshmallows into

Fruit, Vegetable, and Molded Salads

whipped cream and combine with gelatin cubes. Chill several hours before serving.

Makes 12 servings

Note: This salad may be served from large serving bowl or placed into a large loaf pan, frozen, and served when thawed enough to slice.

CARROT AND RAISIN SALAD

2 cups raisins, dry
2 cups grated or shredded carrots

1 cup mayonnaise or salad dressing

Mix together. Chill for at least one hour.
Makes 8 servings.

RAW CAULIFLOWER

1 head cauliflower

Break cauliflower into flowerets, then place in heat-proof jar and pour boiling water over cauliflower. Set aside until cool. Place in refrigerator to chill.

CHERRY SALAD

1 pkg. (6 oz.) cherry gelatin
1 can (1 lb.) pitted bing cherries
1 can (1 lb. 5 oz.) prepared instant cherry pie mix

2 cups very hot water

Dissolve gelatin in water. Pour into 1½-quart mold Add cherries, stir, chill.
Makes 12 servings.

BING CHERRY SALAD

1 pkg. (6 oz.) cherry gelatin
2 cups very hot water
1 can (1 lb.) pitted bing cherries
1 can (15¼ oz.) crushed pineapple (reserve juice from fruit, measure and add enough cold water to make 2 cups)

TOPPING
1 container (4½ oz.) prepared frozen whipped topping or 1 envelope whipped topping, whipped
1 pkg. (3 oz.) cream cheese
½ tsp. lemon juice
3 tbsp. sugar

Dissolve gelatin in hot water. Add juice and water mixture and fruit. Pour into 2-quart mold. Chill to set.
Blend ingredients. Spread over gelatin when it is set.
Makes 12 servings.
Note: Nutmeats and grated cheddar cheese may be sprinkled on top if desired.

MOM'S CABBAGE SALAD

1 head cabbage (medium size), finely chopped
1 can (12 oz.) crushed pineapple

1 pkg. (3 oz.) lime gelatin
1½ cup very hot water
½ cup nutmeats (optional)

Cook cabbage in boiling salted water until barely done (still slightly green). Drain. Dissolve gelatin in very hot water. Add cabbage, pineapple, and nutmeats. Pour into 1½-quart mold. Chill.
Makes 12 servings.

COLE SLAW

½ Cole Slaw Dressing recipe (*see* Index)
1 medium head cabbage

Fruit, Vegetable, and Molded Salads

Cut cabbage in quarters, then grate, grind, or shred. If dressing has been made beforehand, mix well before adding to cabbage. Marinate at least one hour before serving.

Makes 8 servings.

Note: Grated carrots, diced onion, diced green pepper, or drained crushed pineapple may be added to cole slaw if desired. Or grated carrots may be sprinkled around outside edge of serving dish for an attractive garnish.

BACON COLE SLAW

2 small heads cabbage
½ cup grated raw onion
½ cup sugar
½ tsp. salt
¼ tsp. white pepper
2 tbsp. flour
6 strips bacon
4 tbsp. vinegar

Grate cabbage; set aside in heat-proof bowl. Fry bacon until crisp. Remove from pan, crumble. Add onion to bacon fat, frying a few minutes until soft. Add flour and seasonings, and stir until thickened; add vinegar. Return bacon to mixture, and heat to boiling point. Remove from heat, and pour over cabbage. Serve immediately.

Makes 12 servings.

MOLDED COLE SLAW

8 cups grated cabbage
1 pkg. (3 oz.) lemon or lime gelatin
1 cup sugar
½ cup vinegar
½ cup water
1 tsp. salt
1 tsp. celery salt
½ cup mayonnaise or salad dressing

Bring sugar, vinegar, and water to a boil. Remove from heat; add gelatin and seasonings. Let cool. Add mayonnaise. Pour over cabbage. Mix thoroughly. Pour into 1½-quart mold. Chill for at least an hour before serving.

Makes 12 servings.

MACARONI AND HAM COLE SLAW

2 cups elbow macaroni, cooked and cooled
2 cups cooked ham, diced
½ cup sour cream
½ cup mayonnaise or salad dressing
1 tbsp. grated onion
½ tsp. salt
⅛ tsp. white pepper
4 cups shredded cabbage
1 large red apple, diced

Toss ingredients in large bowl. Chill. Let marinate at least one hour before serving.
Makes 8 servings.

RED CABBAGE COLE SLAW

1 head red cabbage
½ cup grape juice
1 cup Cole Slaw Dressing (see Index)

Grate cabbage. Mix grape juice and Cole Slaw Dressing together. Pour over cabbage. Let marinate at least one hour before serving.
Makes 8 servings.

RED CARDINAL COLE SLAW

1 large head cabbage, shredded
1 large red apple, diced
½ cup raisins
½ cup peanuts
1½ cups Cole Slaw Dressing (see Index)

Mix all ingredients. Chill. Let marinate for at least one hour before serving.
Makes 8 servings.

RED AND GREEN COLE SLAW

1 small head red cabbage
1 small head green cabbage
1 cup seedless green grapes, halved
2 oz. blue cheese, crumbled
1¾ cup Cole Slaw Dressing (*see* Index)

Combine ingredients. Chill.
Makes 16 servings.
Let marinate for at least one hour before serving.

Note: Instead of Cole Slaw Dressing, you may mix together:

½ cup vinegar
½ cup mayonnaise or salad dressing
¼ cup granulated sugar
¼ cup powdered sugar
½ cup sour cream

EVERLASTING SALAD

2 heads cabbage, shredded
4 cups cold water
2 green peppers, chopped fine
2 onions, chopped fine
4 carrots, finely grated
1 tbsp. salt
2 tbsp. mustard seed
2 tbsp. celery seed
2 cups vinegar
2 cups sugar

Mix water and salt; pour over cabbage, peppers, onions, and carrots. Let set for 2 hours. Drain.

Mix together seeds, vinegar, and sugar. Heat until sugar dissolves; cool. Pour over cabbage mixture. Let marinate overnight. Will keep for several weeks.

Makes 16 servings.

SWEDISH CABBAGE

2 heads cabbage, quartered and shredded
4 cups sugar
1 cup water
2 cups sweet cider vinegar
1½ tbsp. salt
1 bunch celery, washed and chopped
2 green peppers, diced
2 red pimento peppers, diced
1 tbsp. mustard seed
1 tbsp. celery seed

Cover shredded cabbage with water and salt. Let stand 2 hours.

Squeeze cabbage dry; add celery and green peppers. Mix together sugar, vinegar, and seeds, then pour over vegetables. Set in refrigerator for several days. Will keep at least two weeks.

Makes 16 servings.

CLUB SALAD

1 pkg. (3 oz.) lime gelatin
1 pkg. (3 oz.) lemon gelatin
1 pkg. (3 oz.) cherry, strawberry, or raspberry gelatin
5½ cups very hot water
1 container (4½ oz.) prepared frozen whipped topping or 1 envelope whipped topping, whipped
2 cups miniature marshmallows
1 can (15¼ oz.) crushed pineapple
½ cup sugar
1 pkg. (3 oz.) cream cheese, softened

1. Mix lime gelatin with 2 cups of the water. Pour into pan (9-by-12 inches) and let set until firm.

2. Mix lemon gelatin with 1½ cups of the water. Mix in marshmallows while gelatin is hot, so marshmallows will melt. Cool until gelatin begins to thicken. Stir in 1 cup of the whipped cream, the pineapple, sugar, and cream cheese. Pour mixture over lime gelatin and let set until firm.

3. Mix cherry gelatin with remainder of the hot water. Chill until it begins to thicken; then pour over top of other gelatin. Spread remaining cup of whipped cream over cherry gelatin. Chill until firm.

Makes 16 servings.

Fruit, Vegetable, and Molded Salads

AUNT ARLENE'S COMPLEMENTARY SALAD
(Especially good with fish)

1 pkg. (6 oz.) lemon gelatin
2 cups very hot water
½ cup mayonnaise or salad dressing
1 can (15¼ oz.) crushed pineapple
1 can (11 oz.) mandarin oranges, drained
6 green onions, sliced crosswise very fine, to where the green begins
½ cup minced celery
2 tbsp. chopped chives (frozen, freeze-dried, or fresh)

Dissolve gelatin in very hot water. Cool. Add mayonnaise or salad dressing. Pour into 1½-quart mold. Chill until it begins to thicken. Add remaining ingredients. Chill until set.
Makes 12 servings.

FRESH CRANBERRY SALAD

1 pkg. (1 lb.) fresh cranberries, washed and chopped
1 cup sugar
1 pkg. (6 oz.) cherry gelatin
3 cups very hot water
1 can (15¼ oz.) crushed pineapple
2 cups miniature marshmallows
1½ cup diced celery

Dissolve gelatin in hot water. Add pineapple; pour into 2-quart mold. Chill until almost set. Combine cranberries and sugar with celery, then fold into gelatin. Fold in marshmallows. Chill until firm.
Makes 12 servings.

CRANBERRY HOLIDAY SALAD

1 pkg. (6 oz.) orange gelatin
3 cups very hot water
2 tsp. grated orange rind
1 can (16 oz.) jellied cranberry sauce
1 can (8¾ oz.) crushed pineapple
½ cup diced celery

Dissolve gelatin in hot water, add orange rind, cranberry sauce, and pineapple. Mix together, then add celery. Pour into 1½-quart mold. Chill until firm.

Makes 12 servings.

PARTY CRANBERRY SALAD

1 pkg. (3 oz.) cherry, raspberry, or strawberry gelatin
1 cup very hot water
½ cup cold water
1 can (1 lb.) whole cranberry sauce
1 cup miniature marshmallows

Dissolve gelatin in very hot water. Mix in cranberry sauce, then add cold water; fold in marshmallows. Pour into 1½-quart mold. Chill until firm.

Makes 8 servings.

CRANBERRY SAUCE SALAD

1 can (1 lb.) jellied cranberry sauce
1 cup chopped celery
1 apple, peeled and diced
½ cup chopped walnuts

Cube cranberry sauce, add other ingredients. Toss together. Chill.

Makes 8 servings.

CRYSTAL SALAD

1 pkg. (3 oz.) lemon gelatin
1¼ cup very hot water
½ cup pineapple juice
½ cup mayonnaise or salad dressing
1 small apple, peeled and diced
2 cups whipped cream
1 can (15¼ oz.) pineapple tidbits; drain, reserving ½ cup juice
½ cup diced celery
¾ cup miniature marshmallows
½ cup nutmeats (optional)

Fruit, Vegetable, and Molded Salads 169

Dissolve gelatin in hot water. Add pineapple juice. Chill until slightly congealed, then fold in whipped cream and remaining ingredients. Pour into 1½-quart mold. Chill until firm. Nutmeats may be added if desired.
Makes 8 servings.

CUCUMBER RELISH

2 cucumbers, peeled and grated
2 tbsp. finely chopped green pepper
2 tbsp. finely chopped onion
1 tsp. salt
¼ cup mayonnaise or salad dressing
¼ cup vinegar

Mix together in bowl. Drain before serving.

CUCUMBERS AND ONION RELISH

6 cucumbers
¼ cup pickling salt
4 cups very hot water
3 onions, peeled and sliced

PICKLING MIXTURE
2 cups vinegar
1 cup cold water
½ cup powdered sugar

Peel and slice cucumbers. Let soak in hot salted water while preparing onions. Drain cucumbers. Alternate layers of cucumbers and onions, and cover with Pickling Mixture until well marinated. Drain and serve. Pickling Mixture may be reused for another batch.
Makes 12 servings.

CUCUMBERS IN SOUR CREAM DRESSING

2 cucumbers
1 cup sour cream
2 tbsp. vinegar
1 tbsp. lemon juice
1 tbsp. sugar
1 tsp. salt
⅛ tsp. white pepper
¼ tsp. paprika
½ tsp. dry mustard
1 tsp. celery seeds

Peel and slice cucumbers. Mix all remaining ingredients together in bowl. Add cucumbers. Chill.

Note: Sliced onions may be added to cucumbers. This dressing may be used on cole slaw, zucchini, cauliflower, etc.

EMERALD RELISH

1 pkg. (3 oz.) lime gelatin
¼ tsp. salt
1 cup very hot water
¾ cup cold water
¼ cup vinegar
¼ tsp. salt

⅛ tsp. white pepper
1 tsp. grated onion
2 tbsp. prepared horseradish
1 cucumber, peeled and chopped

Dissolve gelatin and ¼ tsp. salt in hot water. Add cold water and vinegar. Chill.

Mix remaining ingredients together. When gelatin is slightly thickened, fold in mixture. Pour into 1-quart mold. Chill until firm.

Makes 6 servings.

FIVE-CUP FRUIT FANCY

1 can (11 oz.) mandarin oranges, drained
1 can (15¼ oz.) pineapple tidbits, drained; reserve juice
1 cup white seedless grapes, halved

1 cup miniature marshmallows
1 cup sour cream
1 cup coconut (optional)

Combine juice from pineapple with sour cream. Mix with remaining ingredients. Chill.

Makes 12 servings.

FRESH FRUIT SALAD

3 oranges, peeled and sliced
2 grapefruit, peeled and divided into sections
4 bananas, peeled and halved lengthwise
2 cups melon balls
1 pint strawberries, washed, hulled, and cut into halves
1 can (15¼ oz.) pineapple tidbits, drained; reserve juice

Brush banana slices with lemon juice; cut up grapefruit sections and bananas into bite-size pieces.

DRESSING
½ cup pineapple juice from tidbits
1 cup cranberry juice
1 tbsp. cornstarch
2 tbsp. salad oil
2 tbsp. lemon juice
2 tbsp. honey

Blend pineapple juice and cornstarch. Mix with cranberry juice and cook until mixture thickens. Beat in oil, lemon juice, and honey. Chill.

Line a salad bowl with lettuce leaves. Layer and arrange fruit in bowl. Chill. Or arrange on lettuce leaves on individual plates. Chill. Spoon a bit of dressing over salad. Serve remainder in a bowl along with salad.

Makes 20 servings.

LAYERED SALAD

1 head lettuce, shredded as for cole slaw
1 pkg. (10 oz.) frozen green peas
1 cup celery, diced
1 small onion, diced
1 tbsp. sugar
1½ cups mayonnaise or salad dressing
4 oz. cheddar cheese, grated
8 slices bacon, fried crisp, drained and crumbled

Place layer of lettuce in serving pan (approximately 9-by-12 inches) Layer ingredients in order listed above. Chill.

Makes 12 servings.

Note: This salad will keep in the refrigerator for 2 or 3 days.

LETTUCE SALAD

Cut lettuce with stainless steel knife, or tear into bite-sized pieces. Place in salad bowl. Toss with dressing; garnish with any of the following: celery sticks or chopped celery, cauliflower flowerets, grated carrots, grated red cabbage, chinese cabbage, sliced cucumbers, endive, escarole, ripe olives, sliced or chopped onion, red onion rings, red or green pepper rings or diced pepper, sliced red radishes, halved cherry tomatoes, tomato wedges, romaine, sliced hard-cooked eggs, imitation bacon.

Note: For crisp lettuce *see* Hints.

SPICY PEACH SALAD

6 canned peach halves	1 tsp. ground cloves
1 cup syrup from peaches	1 tsp. cinnamon
¼ cup vinegar	¼ tsp. salt
¼ cup brown sugar	1 pkg. (3 oz.) lemon gelatin

Combine syrup, vinegar, sugar, spices, and salt. Heat to very hot, measure, and add to gelatin; then add enough cold water to make 2 cups liquid. Cool until slightly thickened. Arrange peaches in shallow pan. Pour gelatin over them. Chill until firm. Makes 6 servings.

PEAR SALAD

1 can (1 lb.) pear halves, drained; reserve liquid	1 cup very hot water
1 pkg. (6 oz.) lemon gelatin	2 cups orange juice
	2 tbsp. sugar

Mix gelatin with hot water, add orange juice. Measure pear juice, add enough cold water to make 1 cup. Add to gelatin. Chill. Arrange pears in flat shallow pan. When mixture is thickened, pour over pears.

Note: Garnish center of pear with cottage cheese, pineapple, maraschino cherry, ripe or green olive if desired.

Makes 6 servings.

PEAR CRANBERRY SALAD

1 can (1 lb.) pear halves, drained; reserve liquid
2 cups fresh cranberries
½ cup sugar
1 tsp. grated lemon peel

Combine pear syrup with cranberries, sugar, and lemon peel. Bring to boil; simmer 5 minutes. Slice pears, add to mixture and simmer 5 more minutes.
Serve warm or chilled as meat accompaniment.
Makes 6 servings.

PERFECTION SALAD

1 pkg. (3 oz.) celery or mixed vegetable gelatin
1 cup very hot water
2 tsp. vinegar
1 cup minus 2 teaspoons crushed ice and water
½ cup shredded cabbage
½ cup shredded carrot
¼ cup diced celery
1 tbsp. chopped green pepper
1 tsp. chopped pimento (optional)
½ tsp. salt

Dissolve gelatin in hot water. Add vinegar and the ice water. Stir until ice is dissolved. Add vegetables and salt. Pour into 1-quart mold. Chill until firm.
Makes 8 servings.

PERFECTION RELISH SALAD

1 pkg. (3 oz.) orange gelatin
1 can (15¼ oz.) pineapple tidbits, drained; reserve liquid
¼ cup vinegar
2 cups shredded cabbage
1 can (11 oz.) mandarin oranges, drained
2 tbsp. sweet pickle relish, drained
very hot water

Measure pineapple juice and set aside. Dissolve gelatin in enough very hot water to make 1¾ cups liquid when combined with pineapple juice; then add pineapple juice. Add vinegar; cool to jellylike consistency. Fold in remaining ingredients. Pour into 1½-quart mold. Chill.
Makes 8 servings.

PINK OR GREEN OR ORANGE SALAD

For Green Salad use:
1 pkg. (6 oz.) lime gelatin

For Pink Salad use:
1 pkg. (6 oz.) raspberry, cherry, or strawberry gelatin

For Orange Salad use:
1 pkg. (6 oz.) orange gelatin

Combine dry gelatin with remaining ingredients.

- 1 can (15¼ oz.) crushed pineapple
- 1 container (9 oz.) prepared frozen whipped topping
- 1 container (1 lb.) cottage cheese
- 1 can (11 oz.) mandarin oranges

Makes 16 servings.

BASIC POTATO SALAD

- 3 cups hot boiled potatoes, peeled and cubed
- 3 hard-cooked eggs, chopped
- 1 stalk celery, chopped fine
- 1 small onion, diced
- ¼ cup sweet pickle relish
- ⅔ cup mayonnaise or salad dressing
- 1 tbsp. sugar
- 1 tbsp. prepared mustard
- 2 tbsp. Western-style French dressing
- 1 tsp. salt
- ½ tsp. white pepper

Combine all ingredients while potatoes are warm. Chill before serving.
Makes 8 servings.

GOLDEN-EGG RICH POTATO SALAD

6 cups hot boiled potatoes, peeled and cubed
2 small onions, diced
2 stalks celery, chopped fine
½ cup sweet pickle relish
8 hard-cooked eggs, chopped
¼ tsp. yellow food coloring (optional)
2 tbsp. sugar
2 tbsp. prepared mustard
4 tbsp. Western-style French dressing
2 tsp. salt
1 tsp. white pepper
1½ cups mayonnaise or salad dressing

Method No. 1: Combine all ingredients while potatoes are warm. Chill before serving.

Method No. 2: Combine first 6 ingredients, then mix with one recipe of Old-Fashioned Cooked Salad Dressing (*see* Index). Makes 16 servings.

POTATO SALAD LOAF

3 cups cooked chopped ham, beef, or chicken
3 cups hot boiled potatoes, peeled and cubed
½ cup diced celery
1 small onion, diced
1 tbsp. minced parsley
3 tbsp. sweet pickle relish
1 tsp. salt
2 tbsp. Western-style French dressing
¼ tsp. paprika
1⅓ cups mayonnaise or salad dressing

Combine all ingredients, except meat. Chill for ½ hour. Fold in meat. Pack in slightly oiled salad mold, or use a 9-by-5-by-3-inch loaf pan. Chill. Unmold on lettuce leaf. Garnish with green pepper rings and tomato wedges.

Makes 16 servings.

RASPBERRY SALAD

1 pkg. (6 oz.) raspberry gelatin
2 cups very hot water
1 jar (16 oz.) orange-cranberry relish
1 pkg. (10 oz.) frozen raspberries
1 pt. raspberry sherbet

Add hot water to gelatin; stir until dissolved. Add remaining ingredients; stir until sherbet is dissolved. Chill until set, then spoon out from bowl.
Makes 12 servings.

LIME SALAD

1 pkg. (6 oz.) lime gelatin
1 cup very hot water
1½ cups cottage cheese
1 cup pineapple tidbits, drained; measure and reserve liquid

1 pt. lime sherbet

Dissolve gelatin in hot water. Add enough cold water to pineapple juice to make 1 cup then add to gelatin; stir. Add sherbet, stirring until dissolved. Add pineapple tidbits and cottage cheese. Chill until set, then spoon out from bowl.
Makes 12 servings.

RASPBERRY MARSHMALLOW FRUIT MOLD

1 pkg. (3 oz.) raspberry gelatin
1 cup very hot water
1 can (1 lb. 14 oz.) fruit cocktail, drained; measure and reserve liquid

2 cups miniature marshmallows
½ cup chopped nutmeats

Dissolve gelatin in hot water. Add enough cold water to fruit juice to make 1 cup, then add to gelatin; stir. Add fruit cocktail. Chill for ½ hour. Fold in marshmallows. Pour into 2-quart mold. Chill until firm.
Makes 12 servings.

Fruit, Vegetable, and Molded Salads

SAUERKRAUT SALAD

2 cans (1 lb. 11 oz. each) sauerkraut, drained; reserve 1½ cups liquid
1 small onion, chopped
1 green pepper, chopped fine
1 pimento (optional) or ¼ cup diced pimento
2 stalks celery, chopped
1½ cups sugar

Place sauerkraut juice and sugar in enamel or Teflon saucepan. Heat until sugar is dissolved. Mix other ingredients in bowl. Pour syrup over mixture. Chill. Keeps indefinitely. Makes 16 servings.

SNOWTOP MANDARIN MOLD

Start with snowtop. Dissolve gelatin in hot water. Add mayonnaise or salad dressing and sour cream. Mix thoroughly. Pour into 2-quart round mold. Chill until firm.

SNOWTOP
1 pkg. (3 oz.) lemon gelatin
¼ cup very hot water
¼ cup mayonnaise, or combination of sour cream and salad dressing
½ cup heavy cream, whipped
2 pkg. (3 oz. each) orange gelatin

2 cups very hot water
2 cups miniature marshmallows
2 cans (11 oz. each) mandarin oranges, drained
1 can (15¼ oz.) pineapple tidbits, drained; measure and reserve liquid

Then dissolve gelatin in hot water. Add enough cold water to pineapple juice to make 2 cups; add to gelatin and stir. Chill until slightly thickened. Fold in fruit and marshmallows. Pour into mold on top of "snowtop." Chill until set. Unmold on lettuce leaves before serving.
Makes 12 servings.

WALDORF SALAD

3 tart, red apples, diced
½ cup diced celery
⅔ cup nutmeats

½ cup mayonnaise or salad dressing

Combine ingredients. Serve in lettuce cup. Do not let stand very long before serving.

Makes 6 servings.

ORANGE WALDORF SALAD

1½ cups sour cream
4 tsp. honey
1 tsp. poppy seed
¼ tsp. salt
3 tart, red apples, diced
1 orange, peeled, sectioned, and sections cut into two or three pieces

½ cup chopped dates
½ cup chopped celery
½ cup chopped walnuts
1 cup green seedless grapes, cut in half (optional)

Mix first four ingredients in large mixing bowl. Stir in each apple as it is diced. Fold in remaining ingredients. Chill. Serve in lettuce cup. Garnish with walnut half.

Makes 8 servings.

Part 3
OTHER DELIGHTS FOR THE BUFFET TABLE

10

APPETIZERS

CHICKEN WINGS

20 chicken wings	1 tsp. salt
2 cups flour	4 tbsp. sesame seeds

Disjoint or cut wings into thirds. Throw away tip end or use for stock. Roll in salted flour, then sesame seeds. Place on greased cookie sheet. Bake in preheated oven at 375° about 30 minutes.

CRAB CANAPÉS

FILLING
1 can (7½ oz.) crab meat, drained and flaked
2 tbsp. onion, finely minced
2 tbsp. horseradish
1 pkg. (3 oz.) cream cheese at room temperature
1½ tsp. pimento, minced

Combine ingredients, mix well.

PASTRY
2 sticks prepared pie dough
2 tbsp. onion, finely minced

Prepare pastry according to package instructions; add onion while mixing. Roll out dough to ⅛ inch thickness. Cut into squares about 2-by-2-inches. Place 1 rounded teaspoon of filling on each square. Form pastry into balls around the filling; place seam side down on ungreased cookie sheet. Bake in preheated 400° oven until crisp and browned. Serve hot.

Makes 40 canapés.

DEVILED EGGS

12 hard-cooked eggs
1 tbsp. vinegar
½ tsp. dry mustard
1 tsp. Worcestershire sauce
½ cup mayonnaise or salad dressing
1 tsp. salt
dash white pepper

Carefully cut eggs into halves lengthwise. Remove yolks and mash; add other ingredients to mashed yolks.

Pile yolk mixture into halves of egg whites. Sprinkle with paprika.

STUFFED MUSHROOMS

12 large mushrooms
2 tbsp. butter or margarine
1 tsp. grated onion
2 cups soft bread crumbs
1 tbsp. catsup
1 tsp. chopped parsley
½ tsp. salt
¼ tsp. white pepper
strips of pimento

Wash mushrooms and remove stems. Chop the stems. Melt butter or margarine; add stems and onion, and fry gently for a few minutes. Add crumbs, catsup, and parsley, and mix well. Sprinkle salt and pepper over the caps, then stuff with crumb mixture, to heaping. Place on greased baking sheet. Bake at 425° in preheated oven for 15 minutes until stuffing is browned. Garnish with pimento.

OYSTER COCKTAIL

4 extra select oysters for each cocktail

Prepare as for Shrimp Cocktail (*see* Index.) Oysters are served uncooked.

SHRIMP CANAPÉS

1 pkg. (10 biscuits) refrigerated prepared biscuits
1 lb. shrimp, cooked and chopped
⅓ cup mayonnaise or salad dressing
½ cup cheddar cheese, shredded
3 tbsp. minced onion
1 tbsp. green pepper, minced
1 tsp. salt
3 drops Tabasco sauce
1 tsp. sesame seeds

Bake biscuits according to package directions. Cool and split, returning to baking sheet.

Combine all other ingredients, except sesame seeds. Spread mixture over biscuits. Sprinkle sesame seeds over top. Broil until lightly browned. Serve hot.

Makes 20 canapés.

SHRIMP COCKTAIL

6 shrimp for each cocktail
lettuce leaf
chopped celery
Cocktail Sauce (see Index)

Cook shrimp according to package directions for number of cocktails desired. Chill.

Place lettuce leaf in bottom of sherbet glass; add chopped celery, shrimp; pour sauce over shrimp. Serve.

11

SOUPS AND CHOWDERS

BEAN SOUP

2 cups navy or great northern beans	1 tsp. salt
16 cups water	¼ tsp. white pepper
1 onion, minced	2 tbsp. bacon drippings (optional)
1 carrot, grated or minced	1 tbsp. flour

Wash beans; place in cooking pan with 8 cups water. Bring to boil; set aside to soak overnight or several hours. Rinse. Add 8 cups water and vegetables. Simmer at least two hours. Mix flour with bacon drippings (or cold water); add to soup mixture. Simmer another half hour; adding hot water to bring to consistency desired.

Makes 12 servings.

Note: one cup diced cooked ham may be added for extra goodness the last half hour.

BEEF VEGETABLE SOUP

Use same ingredients as for Beef Stew (*see* Index).

Dice the vegetables, but the beef cubes do not need to be browned. Put vegetables, meat, and 12 cups of water in a kettle and cook about 2 hours.

Makes 12 servings.

CHICKEN AND POTATO CHOWDER

1 (2½-3 lb.) chicken
   water to measure
6 potatoes, peeled and diced
3 onions, chopped
1 cup diced celery
½ tsp. celery salt

1 tsp. salt
½ tsp. seasoned salt
4 tbsp. butter or margarine
3 cups dry milk powder
4 tbsp. flour

Cook chicken in pot in hot water until tender. Remove chicken from pot; bone and cut into cubes. Strain broth to remove any bones; measure and return to pot, adding enough water to make 12 cups.

Add potatoes, onions, celery, and seasonings and cook until tender. Mix flour with dry milk, so it will not lump. Add it, margarine or butter, and chicken to the pot. Simmer (do not boil) for about 10 minutes.

Makes 12 servings.

CLAM CHOWDER

4 slices bacon or salt pork
1 can (10½ oz.) minced clams;
   do not drain
2 tbsp. butter or margarine
1 onion, minced
4 cups water

4 potatoes, cooked and diced
½ tsp. salt
dash white pepper
2 cups powdered milk
chopped parsley (optional)

Cut bacon in ½-inch pieces. Cook bacon until lightly browned; add butter or margarine and onion; fry about 1 minute. Add water, potatoes, salt, and pepper; cook 10 minutes. Add clams and juice and powdered milk. Simmer a few minutes. Sprinkle with parsley. Serve from the pot or in individual bowls.

Makes 8 servings.

FISHERMAN'S CHOWDER

6 slices bacon
1 can (10½ oz.) minced clams
1 cup shrimp, cooked and chopped in small pieces
4 tbsp. butter or margarine
1 onion, minced
10 cups water
6 potatoes, cooked and diced
½ tsp. salt
dash white pepper
1 can (lb.) whole kernel corn
1 can (10¾ oz.) cream of celery soup
1 can (5 oz.) water chestnuts, thinly sliced
4 cups powdered milk
chopped parsley (optional)

Cut bacon in ½-inch pieces. Cook bacon until lightly browned; add butter or margarine and onion; fry one minute.
Add water, potatoes, salt, and pepper; cook 10 minutes.
Add corn, soup, and water chestnuts; cook 5 minutes.
Add clams and shrimp; cook 5 minutes.
Add powdered milk; simmer another 5 minutes.
Sprinkle with parsley. Serve from the pot or in individual bowls.
Makes 12 servings.

OYSTER STEW

1 pint oysters
4 tbsp. butter
½ tsp. salt
¼ tsp. white pepper
2 cups dry milk powder mixed in 4 cups hot water

Place oysters and liquor with butter and seasonings in heavy saucepan. Simmer about 3 minutes. Add milk mixture. Simmer another 3 minutes. Do not boil.
Serve from soup pot or in individual bowls. Sprinkle with paprika, nutmeg, or Parmesan cheese, if desired.

SPLIT PEA SOUP

- 1½ cups green split peas
- 10 cups water
- ham bone
- 2 small carrots, peeled and sliced
- 1 stalk celery, sliced, including top
- 1 onion, sliced
- 1 tbsp. chopped parsley
- ½ tsp. salt
- ¼ tsp. white pepper

Place peas in strainer. Wash under cold water; drain. Place in saucepan with water. Add ham bone and vegetables. Bring to boil; simmer about 1 hour. Remove ham bone; carefully bring potato masher down in pan to mash vegetables. Add any pieces of ham that might be clinging to bone; add seasonings. Serve.

EASY POTATO SOUP

- 6 large potatoes (either raw or precooked in skins)
- 10 cups water
- 1 or 2 onions, diced or grated
- ¼ lb. margarine or butter
- 2 tsp. salt
- 1 tsp. white pepper
- 2 cans (10¾ oz. each) cream of celery soup
- 3 cups dry powdered milk

Peel potatoes before cutting each one in about 8 pieces. Cook in water with onion added for about 20 minutes, or until potatoes will break with potato masher but not dissolve. Add remaining ingredients. Simmer until heated thoroughly. Additional water may be added to consistency that pleases the cook.

VEGETABLE CHOWDER

- 10 cups water
- 2 potatoes, peeled and diced
- 1 onion, peeled and diced
- 2 stalks celery, diced
- 1 green pepper, cut fine
- 1 turnip, peeled and diced
- 1 (1 lb.) can tomatoes
- 2 pkgs. (10 oz.) frozen vegetables
- 1 can (10¾ oz.) cream of celery soup
- 2 tbsp. butter or margarine
- 1 tsp. salt
- 1 tsp. white pepper
- 2½ cups dry powdered milk
- 1 tsp. seasoned salt

Place all the vegetables (fresh and frozen) in hot water. Bring to a boil. Cover; simmer for 45 minutes. Add butter or margarine, seasonings, and dry milk. Cover; do not boil; simmer 15 more minutes. Serve.

FRESH VEGETABLE CHOWDER

- 8 cups water
- 2 potatoes, peeled and diced
- 1 onion, chopped fine
- 2 stalks celery, chopped fine
- 2 carrots, peeled and diced
- 1 green pepper, cut fine
- 1 turnip, peeled and diced
- 2 tomatoes, peeled and quartered
- ½ head cabbage, shredded
- 2 tbsp. butter or margarine
- 1 tsp. salt
- 1 tsp. seasoned salt
- ½ tsp. white pepper
- 2 beef or chicken bouillon cubes

Place all the vegetables in hot water. Bring to boil. Cover; simmer for 45 minutes. Dip out a little of the broth to dissolve bouillon cubes. Return to pot with butter or margarine and seasonings. Cover; simmer another 15 minutes. Serve.

SOUFFLÉS

CHEESE SOUFFLÉ

½ lb. cheese, cheddar or American
4 tbsp. flour
4 tbsp. butter or margarine
1½ cups milk
1 tsp. salt
⅛ tsp. white pepper
6 eggs, separated

In top of double boiler, melt butter, add flour, and blend. Add cheese, milk, and seasonings. Cook about 10 minutes. Remove from heat; add beaten egg yolks one at a time. Slightly cool the mixture while beating egg whites until stiff, then pour mixture slowly into the egg whites, folding together.

Pour into 2-quart greased casserole; bake 1 hour in 350° preheated oven. Be sure oven is hot before placing casserole in oven. Serve immediately.

Makes 4 servings.

CHEESE WITH SEAFOOD OR VEGETABLE SOUFFLÉ

3 tbsp. butter or margarine
2 tbsp. cornstarch
½ tsp. salt
¼ tsp. white pepper
1 cup milk
1 cup cheese, grated
4 eggs, separated
1 cup diced shrimp, or any fish or seafood flaked or diced or 1 cup vegetables,* cooked and diced

---

*Eggplant, cauliflower, carrots, celery, asparagus, green beans, peas, onion, a combination, or leftover vegetables may be used.

Melt margarine or butter in saucepan; add cornstarch, seasonings, milk, and cheese. Cook until thickened. Remove from heat; cool about 5 minutes. Add seafood or vegetables, then egg yolks, slightly beaten, one at a time. Fold in stiffly beaten egg whites. Bake in greased casserole in preheated 350° oven for one hour. Be sure oven is hot before placing casserole in oven. Serve immediately.

Makes 4 servings.

PLAIN SOUFFLÉ

2 tbsp. butter or margarine
2 tbsp. flour
2 cups milk

1 tsp. salt
⅛ tsp. white pepper
4 eggs, separated

In top of double boiler, melt butter, blend in flour, and add milk and seasonings. Cook until thickened. Cool about 10 minutes. Add beaten egg yolks one at a time. Fold in stiffly beaten egg whites and pour into greased casserole. Bake in preheated 325° oven 35 to 40 minutes. Be sure oven is hot when casserole is placed in oven. Serve immediately.

Makes 4 servings.

POTATO SOUFFLÉ

2 medium white potatoes or sweet potatoes
¾ cup hot milk
⅓ cup butter or margarine

1 tsp. grated lemon rind
1 tsp. salt
½ tsp. white pepper
4 eggs, separated

Cook potatoes, peel, and mash, adding hot milk, butter, lemon rind, and egg yolks. Beat egg whites until stiff; fold into potato mixture. Bake in preheated 350° oven for 45 minutes.

Makes 4 servings.

SALMON SOUFFLÉ

1 can (7¾ oz.) salmon, flaked
¼ cup butter or margarine
¼ cup flour
½ tsp. dry mustard
¼ tsp. salt

dash white pepper
1 cup milk
6 eggs, separated
1 tbsp. chopped parsley

In a saucepan, melt butter or margarine; blend in flour and seasonings. Add milk gradually, and cook until thick and smooth, stirring constantly. Remove from heat; cool about 10 minutes. Add egg yolks one at a time, stirring each in with mixture. Add parsley and salmon.

Beat egg whites until stiff. Fold salmon mixture into egg whites. Pour into greased casserole. Bake in preheated 375° oven about 30 minutes. Serve immediately.

Makes 6 servings.

Note: Be sure oven is hot when mixture is placed in oven.

TUNA SOUFFLÉ WITH BACON

1 can (7 oz.) tuna, drained and flaked
6 slices bacon; cooked, drained, and crumbled; reserve drippings
2 tbsp. diced onion
2 tbsp. diced celery

⅛ cup flour
1 cup milk
½ tsp. Worcestershire sauce
¼ tsp. salt
⅛ tsp. white pepper
4 eggs, separated

Sauté onion and celery in bacon drippings a few minutes; stir in flour and mix. Stir in milk. Cook, stirring constantly, until sauce thickens. Remove from heat; stir in bacon; add egg yolks one at a time, seasonings, and tuna. Beat egg whites until stiff; fold into mixture. Pour into greased casserole. Bake in preheated 350° oven for 45 minutes.

Makes 4 servings.

Note: Be sure oven is hot before adding casserole.

TURNIP SOUFFLÉ

1 lb. turnips, cooked and peeled	1 tsp. salt
4 tbsp. butter or margarine, melted	¼ tsp. white pepper
4 tbsp. flour	1 tbsp. grated onion
⅓ cup heavy cream or undiluted evaporated milk	4 eggs, separated

Mash turnips; stir in other ingredients, except egg whites. Beat egg whites until stiff; fold into mixture. Turn into buttered casserole; bake in preheated oven at 350° for 45 minutes. Serve immediately.

Makes 4 servings.

Note: Be sure oven is hot before adding casserole.

13
STUFFING, BREADS, AND DUMPLINGS

APPLE STUFFING FOR GOOSE

1 qt. bread crumbs, dry and coarse
½ cup butter or margarine, melted
1 qt. chopped apple
1 cup chopped celery
1 small onion, chopped

1 tsp. salt
½ tsp. celery salt
⅛ tsp. white pepper
1 tsp. paprika
⅛ tsp. ground cloves
¼ tsp. cinnamon
1 cup hot water

Mix bread crumbs with hot water. Add remaining ingredients. Yield: Stuffing for 8-lb. bird.

APPLE-CORN BREAD STUFFING

6 cups corn bread crumbs (leftover corn bread crumbled) or use 1 pkg. (15 oz.) corn bread mix, cooked according to directions and cooled

1 lb. sausage, cooked and crumbled
3 cups chopped apples
1 cup apple juice
½ tsp. salt

Mix all ingredients together. Yield: Stuffing for 10-lb. bird.

BREAD STUFFING

3 tbsp. butter or margarine, melted	1 tsp. salt
1 tbsp. onion, chopped	½ tsp. sage or poultry seasoning
2 stalks celery, chopped	½ tsp. chopped parsley
3 cups dry bread crumbs	¼ tsp. white pepper
	1 cup milk or stock to moisten

Melt butter in frying pan; add onion and celery; sauté until tender. Combine all ingredients.

This recipe makes a loose light stuffing, preferred by many to the soft moist kind.

Yield: Stuffing for 6-lb. bird.

MOIST BREAD STUFFING

6 cups chopped bread	2 stalks celery, chopped
3 eggs, beaten	1 tsp. salt
2 cups broth	⅛ tsp. white pepper
¼ lb. margarine or butter	¼ tsp. poultry seasoning
3 tbsp. onion, chopped	

Heat broth in saucepan; add onions and celery; simmer for 5 minutes. Add margarine; heat, then pour over chopped bread. Add remaining ingredients.

Yield: Stuffing for 12-lb. bird.

CHESTNUT STUFFING

½ cup butter or margarine, melted	4 cups bread, cubed
2 small onions, chopped	1 tsp. salt
1 stalk celery, diced	½ tsp. white pepper
1 lb. chestnuts, cooked and coarsely cut	

Stuffing, Breads, and Dumplings

Melt butter or margarine; slowly cook onions and celery until golden brown. Add remaining ingredients. Mix until all ingredients are blended. Use as stuffing, or cook in greased casserole to be served with entree.

To cook chestnuts: Slash chestnut and toss into boiling water. Boil 20 minutes; peel while hot. Chop or cut into small pieces.

Yield: Stuffing for 10-lb. bird.

CHIVE AND WILD RICE STUFFING FOR GAME

1 cup wild rice, cooked
⅓ cup celery, chopped fine
2 tbsp. butter or margarine
¼ lb. bacon or fat from ham
1 tsp. salt
1 can (3 oz.) sliced mushrooms
1 can (5 oz.) water chestnuts, grated or chopped
3 tbsp. chopped chives, frozen, freeze-dried, or fresh
¼ cup chopped walnuts
1 tsp. poultry seasoning
1 egg, slightly beaten
giblets, chopped (optional)

Prepare wild rice according to Quick-Soak Method (*see* Index). Cook in covered saucepan about 25 minutes.

Prepare game bird for roasting. Place butter in skillet. Sauté bacon, giblets, celery, water chestnuts for 5 minutes. Remove from heat. Mix all remaining ingredients together. Stuff the bird.

Yield: Stuffing for 6-lb. bird.

OYSTER STUFFING

1 pint oysters
½ cup melted butter
4 cups soft bread crumbs
1½ tsp. salt
½ tsp. white pepper

Drain oysters; cut in half. Measure liquor; if there is not ¼ cup add enough water to make that amount. Mix everything together. Use as stuffing for poultry or game bird, or cook in greased casserole in oven with the bird.

Yield: Stuffing for 8-lb. bird.

BANANA-DATE-NUT BREAD

1¾ cups flour	1 cup bananas, mashed (2-3)
1¼ tsp. baking powder	¼ tsp. banana flavor extract
½ tsp. baking soda	1 box (14 oz.) prepared date bread mix
¾ tsp. salt	
⅓ cup shortening	1 box (14 oz.) prepared nut bread mix
⅔ cup sugar	
4 eggs, slightly beaten	2 cups water

Put everything, but bananas in a large mixing bowl. (Add mixes without adding water or eggs; they are included in recipe.) Mix well. Fold in bananas. Do not whip with beater after adding bananas.

Bake in 3 loaf pans in preheated 350° oven for 50 minutes to 1 hour.

GARLIC BREAD

1 loaf Italian or French bread	½ lb. butter or margarine, softened
1½ tsp. garlic powder	

Slice bread crosswise at 1-inch intervals, but not through completely. Spread each side with the butter or margarine mixed with the garlic powder. Lay bread on piece of aluminum foil, and fold foil tightly at the top. Heat in preheated 400° oven for 15 minutes. Serve in foil, partially unwrapped, to keep warm.

YORKSHIRE PUDDING

1 cup milk	¼ tsp. salt
½ cup flour	beef fat and broth from roast
2 eggs	

Stuffing, Breads, and Dumplings

Mix salt and flour; add milk gradually to form a smooth paste, then add eggs, beaten two minutes using an egg beater. Heat beef broth in 9-by-12 inch baking pan; pour mixture in pan. Place in preheated 400° oven for 30 minutes. Cut in squares and serve on plate around roast.

Makes 4 servings.

CORN BREAD

1¼ cups yellow cornmeal
¾ cup flour
1 tbsp. baking soda
½ tsp. salt

1 egg
1 cup milk
¼ cup vegetable oil

Sift dry ingredients into bowl. Add egg, milk, and oil. Beat until smooth.

Bake in greased 8-inch baking pan in preheated 425° oven for 20 or 25 minutes.

Note: For muffins, mix as above; use 12-cup pan; bake in preheated 425° oven for 15 minutes.

FRIED CORNMEAL MUSH

2 cups milk
1 cup hot water
1 cup cold water

1 cup yellow cornmeal
1 tsp. salt

Mix milk and hot water in a large saucepan, and bring to boil. Mix cold water, cornmeal, and salt. Pour into boiling mixture, stirring constantly; cook until thickened.

Pour mush into greased loaf pan; chill for several hours or overnight.

When mush is cold, cut into ½-inch slices; dip in flour or cornmeal; fry in very hot fat on both sides. Serve hot with syrup.

Makes 4 servings.

HUSH PUPPIES

1 cup yellow cornmeal
⅓ cup flour, sifted
1 tsp. salt
1 tsp. baking powder

½ tsp. soda
½ cup minced onion
¾ cup milk

Stir ingredients together. Mix well. Drop by teaspoons into hot fat in electric skillet set at 375°. Fry a few at a time until golden. Drain on absorbent paper.
Makes 8 servings.

DUMPLINGS

2 cups flour
1 tsp. salt
4 tsp. baking powder
¼ tsp. white pepper

1 egg, well beaten
3 tbsp. melted butter
¾ cup milk

Sift dry ingredients together. Add egg, butter, milk; mix well. Drop by teaspoons into boiling liquid. Use kettle with wide bottom, with not over an inch of liquid in bottom of kettle.

Cover; cook 10 minutes without removing cover. Remove cover; cook another 10 minutes. Add to entree.
Yield: 16 dumplings.

QUICK DUMPLINGS

2 cups prepared biscuit mix

1 egg, well beaten in cup.

Use the beaten egg as part of required milk called for on instructions on box. Cook the same as method for Dumplings.
Yield 16 dumplings.

14

SAUCES

SAUCES

Sauces are a must for many buffet foods. Use sauce for creamed vegetables, for basting, for dipping, to serve with meats, fish, and vegetables on the buffet table. Sauces that are served hot may be used for fondue dips.

ANCHOVY SAUCE

1 can (2 oz.) anchovy fillets, minced
½ tsp. garlic powder
1 cup tomato juice
½ cup butter
juice of 1 lemon

Combine all ingredients in saucepan. Simmer until butter is melted.

Note: Use as a basting sauce for fish, a dip for chips or vegetables, a hot or cold dip for beef fondue.

APPLESAUCE GLAZE

2 cups applesauce
½ cup orange marmalade
1 tsp. prepared mustard
⅛ tsp. cinnamon

Mix together.

Note: Use as a basting sauce for beef or ham; spoon over grilled pork chops.

BARBECUE SAUCE

2 tbsp. butter or margarine
2 cups crushed pineapple
½ cup lemon juice
1 tbsp. bottled browning and seasoning sauce
1 large onion, chopped fine
1 tbsp. vinegar
1 tsp. salt
½ tsp. celery salt
1 tbsp. barbecue spice
2 drops liquid smoke (optional)
1 cup water
4 cups catsup
2 cups brown sugar

Mix all ingredients, except catsup and brown sugar, in a saucepan. Heat to boiling. Add catsup and brown sugar; simmer a few minutes.

Note: Use as a sauce in which to serve cooked pork, beef, or chicken. Use as a basting sauce for oven or grill cooking for meats.

BROWN GRAVY

6 tbsp. flour
4 tbsp. frying fat
2 cups liquid (cold stock or water or milk or any combination)
salt
pepper
1 tsp. bottled browning and seasoning sauce

Cook flour in fat in skillet, stirring constantly. Just before it is about to scorch, add the liquid. Cook, stirring constantly, until thickened.

Note: Serve as gravy. Use as a sauce for meatballs, cooked beef, pork, or chicken. Add a can of cream of mushroom soup; heat; serve over cooked hamburger patties.

CHEESE SAUCE

4 tbsp. butter or margarine
4 tbsp. flour
1 tsp. salt
2 cups milk
8 slices cheddar cheese, broken into pieces

In top of double boiler, melt butter or margarine; add flour; mix. Add other ingredients, and cook until thickened.

Note: Use as a sauce over baked potato or cooked cauliflower. Serve as a dip for bread fondue.

COCKTAIL SAUCE

2 cups catsup
½ tsp. horseradish
2 tbsp. lemon juice

1 drop Tabasco sauce
dash salt

Mix together.

Note: Use as a dipping sauce for cooked shrimp, breaded French-fried shrimp, oysters, or scallops. Use as a sauce for hot lobster in place of butter. Pour over seafood cocktails.

CREOLE SAUCE

½ cup butter or margarine
1 onion, chopped
1 green pepper, chopped
2 cups tomatoes, whole peeled, or tomato juice
1 tbsp. sugar

¼ tsp. crushed oregano
1 can (8 oz.) tomato paste plus 1 can water
1 tsp. salt
¼ tsp. white pepper
¼ tsp. celery salt

In a heavy saucepan, melt butter or margarine; sauté onion and green pepper until limp. Add remaining ingredients. Cook for 15 minutes.

Note: 1. Pour over cooked whole kernel corn, cooked celery, green or regular lima beans after cooking, or cooked shrimp.

2. To cook (8 oz.) macaroni or spaghetti, add 5 cups hot water to sauce and boil about 10 minutes.

3. Use as a sauce for cooked turtle. Add 1 can (10 ¾ oz.) cream of celery soup to sauce; add cooked turtle. (This is the sauce that is used for the turtle on the Buffet.)

CRIMSON GLAZE

4 tbsp. catsup
3 tbsp. margarine

1 tbsp. sweet pickle relish

Combine and heat until margarine melts.
Note: Use as a glaze while broiling fish.

CUSTARD SAUCE

1 egg
1 cup milk
½ tsp. vanilla

2 tbsp. sugar
⅛ tsp. salt

Whip together; cook in top of double boiler until thickened. Chill.
Note: Use as a topping for any kind of pudding, gelatin dessert, or gingerbread. Use as a filling for jelly roll.

DILL SAUCE

½ cup sour cream
⅓ cup chili sauce
1 tsp. lemon juice
¼ tsp. dill weed crushed

2-3 drops Tabasco sauce
dash onion salt
dash celery salt
dash white pepper

Combine ingredients. Chill.
Note: Use as a dipping sauce.

DIPPING SAUCE

2 cups mayonnaise or salad dressing
1 cup chili sauce
¾ cup sour cream

½ cup chicken consomme
2 tbsp. green pepper, diced
1 tbsp. lemon juice
2 tsp. anchovy paste

Sauces

Combine all ingredients. Mix well. Chill.
Note: Use as dipping sauce for vegetables, cold lobster, crabmeat, shrimp, and salmon.

FOAMY SAUCE

3 tbsp. butter or margarine
1 cup powdered sugar
2 eggs, separated

½ tsp. vanilla
1 cup heavy cream, whipped

Combine in top of double boiler butter, sugar, egg yolks. Cook until blended. Remove from heat; fold in beaten egg whites; continue beating; add vanilla. Fold in whipped cream.
Note: Use as a topping for gingerbread, fruit, pudding, and sponge cake.

HARD SAUCE

½ cup butter or margarine
1 cup powdered sugar

¼ tbsp. lemon juice
2 tsp. vanilla

Cream butter; add sugar gradually; add lemon juice and vanilla. Chill. Serve cold.
Note: Use as a complementary sauce for puddings, whether served warm or cold, or as a topping for gingerbread.

HAWAIIAN MARINADE

½ cup sweet cider vinegar
⅔ cup cooking oil
2 tsp. salt
½ tsp. white pepper

1 onion, minced
1½ cups unsweetened pineapple juice

Blend together all ingredients.
Note: Use to marinate lobster tails, pork chops, fresh ham, or pork shoulder, and as basting sauce during cooking.

HOLLANDAISE SAUCE

¼ cup butter or margarine, melted and kept warm
2 egg yolks
dash salt
dash white pepper
⅓ cup very hot water
1 tsp. lemon juice

Put about 1 inch of water in bottom half of a double boiler so that it will not touch the top half. Place egg yolks in top of double boiler; beat a few minutes while cooking. Add hot water, melted butter, seasonings, and lemon juice very slowly while constantly whipping. Do not boil. Remove from heat when thickened. Serve immediately.

Note: Use with broccoli, asparagus, or artichoke.

HORSERADISH SAUCE

½ cup sour cream
½ tsp. salt
¼ cup horseradish
1½ tbsp. tarragon vinegar

Combine ingredients. Mix well. Chill.

Note: Serve with ham.

LEMON-GARLIC BUTTER

½ cup butter or margarine
¼ tsp. garlic powder
2 tsp. flour
⅓ cup water
3 tbsp. lemon juice
4 tsp. sugar
½ tsp. salt
⅛ tsp. white pepper

Melt butter in saucepan and add flour, blending until smooth. Remove from heat; stir in remaining ingredients. Cook over low heat, stirring constantly, until thickened.

Note: Use as a basting sauce for seafoods, or serve in warmer as a dip for fondue.

MINCEMEAT LEMON SAUCE

1 pkg. (9 oz.) mincemeat, dried
½ cup water

½ cup lemon juice

Break mincemeat in small pieces in saucepan. Add water; place over medium heat; stir until lumps are dissolved. Boil for one minute. Stir in lemon juice.
Note: Serve warm with ham.

MUSTARD SAUCE

1 cup mayonnaise or salad dressing
2 tbsp. prepared mustard
¼ cup green onion, chopped from root to end of white

3 drops Tabasco sauce
½ tsp. dry mustard

Mix ingredients. Chill.
Note: Serve as a relish for ham, roast beef, or cold fish. It may also be served as a dip for beef fondue.

ORANGE-BUTTER SAUCE

1 can (6 oz.) frozen orange juice, undiluted
¼ cup lemon juice
½ tsp. dry mustard

½ tsp. celery salt
½ tsp. salt
½ tsp. onion powder
½ cup melted butter

Combine all ingredients in saucepan, except butter. Heat slowly until mixture comes to a boil. Boil 1 minute; add butter.
Note: Use as basting sauce for duck, a hot sauce dip for cocktail seafoods, a hot sauce when lobster is served, or as a dipping sauce (kept warm) for fondue.

PARSLEY-BUTTER FOR SEAFOOD OR POTATOES

¼ cup butter or margarine
1 tsp. lemon juice

1 tbsp. parsley, finely chopped
¼ tsp. salt

Melt butter; blend in remaining ingredients.
Note: Serve as warm dip, or pour over seafood or potatoes.

PIQUANT SAUCE

2 tbsp. butter or margarine
2 tbsp. flour
2 cups beef consomme
¼ cup green onions, chopped; from root to end of white
¼ cup pickle, chopped (either sweet or dill)

1 tbsp. chopped capers
1 tsp. chopped chervil
1 tbsp. chopped parsley
1 bay leaf
dash salt
dash white pepper

Melt butter or margarine in saucepan; sauté onions until slightly browned. Remove from heat; stir in flour and mix until blended. Add all other ingredients. Simmer over very low heat about 15 minutes. Strain.
Note: Use to spice up bland foods such as veal, eggs, or fish.

ROQUEFORT OR BLUE CHEESE SAUCE

1 pkg. (4 oz.) Roquefort or blue cheese, crumbled
1½ cup salad oil
½ cup lemon juice

1 tsp. salt
1 tsp. paprika
½ tsp. white pepper

Place ingredients in blender or shake in jar, until well mixed.
Note: Use as a basting sauce or dip.

SOUR CREAM CHIVE FOR BAKED POTATO

1 box (8 oz.) sour cream
8 oz. cottage cheese
1 tsp. onion, minced

½ tsp. horseradish
1 tbsp. chopped chives

Combine ingredients and serve over baked potato.
Note: Mix 1 pkg (1¼ oz.) dry onion soup mix with above, and use for dipping sauce.

SPANISH SAUCE

2 onions, sliced
4 tbsp. cooking oil
2½ cups canned tomatoes or tomato juice
1 small green pepper, diced

1 bay leaf
3 whole cloves
1 tbsp. sugar
3 tbsp. flour
¼ cup water

Cook onion slowly in cooking oil; add green pepper; cook about 1 minute. Blend flour with water, and add along with all remaining ingredients. Simmer 15 minutes. Remove bay leaf and cloves before serving.
Note: Serve over cooked spaghetti or macaroni, or use as a sauce for meat or fish on the buffet table.

SWEET-SOUR SAUCE

¼ cup cornstarch
¼ cup brown sugar
⅓ cup soy sauce

½ cup vinegar
2 cups water, soup stock, or pineapple juice

Mix ingredients in a saucepan. Heat, stirring constantly, until thick and clear.
Note: Use for pork steak, pork ribs, or as a basting sauce.

TARTAR SAUCE

1 cup mayonnaise or salad dressing
½ cup sweet pickle relish, well drained, or sweet pickle, diced

1 tsp. onion, minced
1 tbsp. lemon juice

Combine ingredients. Chill.
Note: Serve with seafood.

VELOUTÉ SAUCE

Make White Sauce recipe (*see* Index); use stock from meat or fish instead of milk.

WELSH RAREBIT

1 tbsp. butter or margarine
½ lb. cheese American or cheddar, cut in small pieces
½ cup milk
1 tsp. Worcestershire sauce
½ tsp. dry mustard
½ tsp. salt
white pepper

Melt butter or margarine in double boiler. Add cheese, milk, and seasoning. Cook until cheese is melted and mixture is well blended. Pour over hot toast; serve immediately.
Makes 4 servings.

WHITE SAUCE

THIN SAUCE:
1 tbsp. butter or margarine
1 tbsp. flour
½ tsp. salt
1 cup milk
MEDIUM SAUCE:
2 tbsp. butter or margarine
2 tbsp. flour
½ tsp. salt
1 cup milk
THICK SAUCE:
4 tbsp. butter
4 tbsp. flour
½ tsp. salt
1 cup milk

In top of double boiler, melt butter, add flour, and blend. Add milk gradually, stirring constantly. Cook until thickened. Add salt.
Note: 1. Use as buffet serving sauce for vegetables or codfish or dried beef, or serve as a gravy (other seasonings may be added). It is the basis of gravy for creamed new potatoes and peas.
2. For cheese sauce for fondue, make medium sauce, adding 4 slices of cheese.
3. Combine with 1 can (10 ¾ oz.) cream of celery or cream of mushroom soup for a delicious cream sauce.

15

SALAD DRESSINGS

BLUE CHEESE OR ROQUEFORT SALAD DRESSING

1 pkg. (4 oz.) Roquefort or blue cheese

1 quart mayonnaise or salad dressing

Crumble cheese in bowl. Add mayonnaise or salad dressing. Mix lightly. Refrigerate. Serve on lettuce salad.

CELERY SEED DRESSING

1 tsp. salt
1 tsp. dry mustard
1 tsp. paprika
1 tbsp. celery seed

½ cup light corn syrup
⅓ cup vinegar
1 cup vegetable oil
1 tbsp. onion, grated

Beat all ingredients together in a small bowl until well blended and thickened. Chill. Shake before using.

COLE SLAW DRESSING

1 cup sour cream
1 cup mayonnaise or salad dressing
1 cup granulated sugar

1 cup powdered sugar
1 cup sweet cider vinegar
½ tsp. salt

Combine ingredients in a bowl. Mix with electric mixer or egg beater. Pour into a jar. This dressing will keep several weeks in refrigerator.

Note: You may use the 8-ounce container of sour cream for the measure.

OLD-FASHIONED COOKED SALAD DRESSING

2 eggs
1 cup milk
⅓ cup sugar
3 tbsp. flour
1½ tsp. salt
¼ tsp. white pepper
1½ tsp. dry mustard
¼ tsp. paprika
1 tbsp. lemon juice
⅓ cup vinegar

Put all ingredients except vinegar in heavy saucepan. Whip until smooth. Cook slowly over low heat, stirring constantly, until thickened. Stir in vinegar.

FRUIT SALAD DRESSING

¼ cup light corn syrup
½ cup sour cream
½ cup mayonnaise or salad dressing

Mix until smooth. Chill. Pour over salad of fresh or canned fruit.

POPPY SEED DRESSING

⅓ cup vinegar
1 tsp. salt
¾ cup sugar
½ tsp. dry mustard
1 cup vegetable oil
1 tbsp. onion, finely grated
2 tbsp. poppy seed

Put vinegar, sugar, salt, and mustard in a mixing bowl. Slowly add oil, mixing with electric mixer. Blend in onion and poppy seed. Chill. Shake before serving.

Salad Dressings

HERBED SOUR CREAM DRESSING

1 cup bottled herb salad dressing
2 cups sour cream

Combine. Chill.
Note: Use as a salad dressing, or serve as relish for seafood.

THOUSAND ISLAND DRESSING

2 cups mayonnaise or salad dressing
½ cup Western-style French dressing
½ cup sweet pickle relish
12 stuffed olives, diced

Mix ingredients together. Chill.

WORLD WAR II HOMEMADE MAYONNAISE

2 egg yolks
1 tsp. dry mustard
½ tsp. salt
¼ tsp. white pepper
1 tbsp. sugar
4 tbsp. vinegar or lemon juice
2 cups vegetable oil

Place all ingredients except oil in a mixing bowl. Use electric mixer; add oil drop by drop at first, gradually increasing amount until all is used. Chill before serving.

16

DESSERTS

APPLESAUCE

2 (25 oz.) jars canned applesauce or 2 quarts freshly made applesauce	1 tsp. cinnamon
	⅛ tsp. nutmeg
½ cup brown sugar	dash allspice
½ cup granulated sugar	dash pumpkin pie spice
	dash apple pie spice

Add sugar and spices to hot cooked applesauce, or heat 1 cup canned applesauce in saucepan with sugar and spices. Mix with remainder of applesauce.

Makes 12 servings.

BAKED APPLES

Select firm, medium-sized baking apples. (Your grocer will be happy to advise which apples in stock are best for baking.) Wash apples, and remove core with vegetable peeler or apple corer. Peel skin from stem end to about ¼ inch past the curve.

Fill each cavity with two tablespoons white or brown sugar. Add a sprinkling of lemon juice, a dash of cinnamon, and a dot of butter.

Place in casserole or baking dish with cover. Add about ¼ inch of water in the bottom of the dish. Bake in preheated 375° oven, covered, about 40 minutes.

Remove apples to individual serving plates; pour and divide any remaining syrup in pan over apples. Cream or whipped cream may be served with apples.

BERRY REFRIGERATOR DESSERT

CRUST
1½ cups graham cracker crumbs
3 tbsp. sugar
½ cup melted butter
BERRY FILLING
2 pkgs. (10 oz. each) frozen raspberries or strawberries
1 cup water
½ cup sugar

2 tsp. lemon juice
4 tbsp. cornstarch dissolved in ¼ cup cold water
MARSHMALLOW FILLING
1 cup miniature marshmallows, preferably white
1 cup milk
1 container (4½ oz.) prepared whipped topping

To prepare crust: Blend ingredients in a 9-by-13-inch baking pan. Press in bottom of pan. Bake at 350° for 10 minutes. Cool thoroughly.

To prepare berry filling: Place water, sugar, lemon juice, and cornstarch mixture in a saucepan; cook until thickened and clear; add berries; mix lightly; set aside to cool.

To prepare marshmallow filling: Melt marshmallows in milk in top of double boiler. Cool thoroughly. Fold in the whipped topping, then spread over crumb crust. Spread berry mixture over marshmallow mixture. Refrigerate until firm.

Makes 12 servings.

BERRY REFRIGERATOR DESSERT II

CRUST
½ cup plus 1 tbsp. margarine or butter
1 cup flour
1 tbsp. sugar
CHEESE FILLING
2 pkgs. (3 oz. each) cream cheese, softened
2 cups powdered sugar
½ tsp. salt

2 tsp. vanilla
1 pkg. (1½ oz.) whipped topping mix, whipped
BERRY FILLING
1 pkg. (6 oz.) raspberry or strawberry gelatin
2½ cups very hot water
2 pkgs. frozen raspberries or strawberries, thawed
½ cup sugar

Desserts

To prepare crust: Combine ingredients; press into 9-by-13-inch baking pan. Bake 20 minutes in preheated 300° oven. Cool.

To prepare cheese filling: Cream together cheese, powdered sugar, vanilla, and salt. Fold in whipped cream, adding slowly at first. Spread over crust and chill.

To prepare berry filling: Dissolve gelatin in hot water; add sugar; stir in fruit. Chill until partially thickened. Pour over cheese mixture. Chill several hours or overnight.

Makes 12 servings.

BREAD PUDDING

1 loaf bread, or equivalent in stale bread or rolls
4 cups hot water
⅛ lb. butter or margarine
1⅓ cups dry powdered milk
½ cup sugar
⅓ cup brown sugar
2 tsp. cinnamon
⅛ tsp. allspice
⅛ tsp. nutmeg
⅛ tsp. pumpkin pie spice
⅛ tsp. apple pie spice
1 can (1 lb.) applesauce, apricots, or pears, or equivalent in fresh fruit (if apricots or pears are used, chop very fine or put in blender and liquefy)
4 eggs, beaten
whipping cream or cream

Crumble bread; pour hot water over bread. Add butter or margarine; let stand a few minutes. Mash with potato masher. Add dry powdered milk, sugar, and seasonings; add beaten egg. Mix well. Pour into greased casserole; bake 50 minutes in preheated 350° oven. Serve with whipped cream or pour cream over top. Serve warm.

Makes 12 servings.

Note: If using a microwave oven, bake 10 minutes; stir; bake 5 more minutes.

CHERRY-CHOCOLATE TREAT

1 box prepared chocolate cake mix	2 cans (1 lb. 5 oz.) prepared instant cherry pie mix

Prepare cake according to package directions. Bake in two pie pans. Cool.

Place one layer of cake on large cake plate; spread liberally with one of the cans of pie mix.

Place the second layer on top; add second can of cherry pie mix. Cut in pie shaped wedges. (If you are economically minded, use only one can.)

Makes 12 servings.

Note: 1. For variety, use a white cake mix and put strawberry, blueberry, or cherry pie mix on the white layers.

2. For a quick treat, bake in microwave oven. Bake each half in glass pie pan a total of 10 minutes, turning pan every 2 minutes. Bake each pan separately

CHOCOLATE ÉCLAIRS

½ cup butter or margarine	⅛ tsp. salt
1 cup boiling water	3 cups hot water
½ tsp. salt	1 cup dry powdered milk
1 cup flour, sifted	1 tsp. vanilla flavoring
4 eggs	FROSTING
FILLING	1 square unsweetened chocolate
3 squares unsweetened chocolate	2 tbsp. milk
5 tbsp. cornstarch	2 cups powdered sugar, sifted
½ cup sugar	1 tsp. vanilla

Melt butter in top of double boiler; bring to a boil; lower heat. Add salt and flour, stirring rapidly, until mixture leaves sides of pan and gathers around spoon in a smooth compact mass. Remove from heat.

Desserts

Add 1 egg at a time, beating thoroughly after each addition. Continue beating until mixture looks satiny and breaks off when spoon is raised.

Drop rounded tablespoons every 6 inches in rows about 2½ inches apart on ungreased baking sheets. With spatula, spread each mound into a rectangle about 4 inches long and 1 inch wide, rounding sides and piling dough on top. Bake in preheated 400° oven for 40 minutes, or until puffed, dry, and golden brown. Cool on rack. (Use oven rack.)

When cool, cut éclair lengthwise without separating; as a baked potato would be cut. Place filling between halves.

Spread tops with chocolate frosting.

To make filling: Shave chocolate and place in top of double boiler. Stir in cornstarch, sugar, salt. Add hot water and powdered milk. Stir constantly until thick and smooth. Add vanila. Or leave out the chocolate, and cook filling same way.

To make frosting: Shave and melt chocolate in top of double boiler; add milk, powdered sugar, and vanilla. Remove from heat; finish blending until mixture has a spreading consistency. Spread over éclair.

Place in refrigerator until ready to serve, or store in freezer. Makes 12 éclairs.

HEAVENLY HASH

2 cups cooked rice, cold
1 cup crushed pineapple
1 cup whipped cream
1 cup miniature marshmallows

Combine ingredients. Chill.
Makes 8 servings.

Note: For added flavor, cook rice in fruit juice or maraschino cherry juice.

INDIAN PUDDING

3 cups milk
½ cup yellow cornmeal
1 tbsp. butter or margarine
½ cup molasses

½ tsp. salt
½ tsp. ginger
1 cup cold milk

In top of double boiler scald 2 cups of the milk. Mix cornmeal and 1 cup of milk; combine with scalded milk. Cook for 25 minutes, stirring frequently.

Stir in remaining ingredients, except cold milk. Pour mixture into 2-quart greased casserole, then pour cold milk over top.

Set casserole in deep roasting pan in oven. Pour boiling water around casserole to within 1 inch of the top of the casserole. Bake covered in preheated 300° oven for 1 hour. Uncover; bake 1 more hour. Serve warm with ice cream or whipped cream topping.

Makes 6 servings.

QUICK JELLY ROLL DOUGH

1½ cups pancake mix
½ cup sugar
½ cup milk
1 egg

¼ cup butter or margarine
1 cup jelly or Custard Sauce
 (see Index)

Combine ingredients in bowl and mix. Handle as for jelly roll dough. Bake on 10½-by-15½-inch cookie sheet in a preheated 425° oven about 10 minutes. Remove from oven; cool about 5 minutes; turn on cloth towel; spread with jelly or cream or custard filling. Roll as a paper towel is rolled; place seam on bottom; wrap towel around jelly roll to secure while cooling.

Makes 12 servings.

Note: For cupcakes, divide dough in 12 muffin tins with 1 heaping teaspoon of mincemeat on top. Bake in preheated 425° oven for 15-20 minutes.

SHOOFLY PIE

1 cup sifted all-purpose flour
¼ cup light brown sugar, firmly packed
½ tsp. salt
½ tsp. cinnamon
⅛ tsp. nutmeg
⅛ tsp. ground cloves
2 tbsp. soft margarine
½ tsp. baking soda
½ cup molasses
¾ cup hot water
1 unbaked 9-inch pie shell
vanilla ice cream

In mixing bowl, combine baking soda and hot water. Stir in remaining ingredients. Pour into pie shell. Bake in preheated oven at 375° for 30 minutes. Serve warm with vanilla ice cream over top.

Makes 6 servings.

IRISH COFFEE

Irish whiskey
hot strong black coffee
whipped cream
sugar

Pour 1 shot glass of whiskey in bottom of each cup. Fill cup with coffee to within ½ inch of top. Float a heaping tablespoon of whipped cream on top of coffee.

Serve sugar on the side.

TITLE INDEX

A Buncha Chili for a Buncha People, 36
Acorn Squash, 129
Anchovy Sauce, 201
Apple-Corn Bread Stuffing, 196
Apple Salad, 155
Applesauce, 215
Applesauce Glaze, 201
Apple Stuffing for Goose, 196
Apricot Fizz Salad, 156
Aunt Arlene's Complementary Salad, 167
Avocado on the Half Shell, 157

Bacon Cole Slaw, 163
Baked Apples, 215
Baked Beans, 102
Baked Hubbard Squash, 130
Baked Broccoli, 107
Baked Corned Beef Hash, 25
Baked Onions, 119
Baked Pheasant, 77
Baked Pheasant with Rice, 78
Baked Pork Chops, 51
Baked Pork Chops with Apples, 52
Baked Squash with Apple, 128
Banana-Apricot Salad, 158
Banana-Date-Nut Bread, 198
Banana Salad, 157
Barbecue Sauce, 202
Barbecued Chicken, 63
Barbecued Pork Chops, 52
Barbecued Ribs, 56
Barbecued Shrimp, 99
Basic Directions for Cooking South African Rock Lobster Tails, 92
Basic Potato Salad, 174
Bean Soup, 185
Bean Sprout Salad, 158
Beans and Sprouts, 104
Beef and Noodles, 21
Beef Souper, 21
Beef Stew, 22
Beef Stroganoff, 25
Beef Vegetable Soup, 185
Beet-Onion Casserole, 107
Berry Refrigerator Dessert, 216
Bing Cherry Salad, 162
Blue Cheese or Roquefort Salad Dressing, 211
Boiled Onions in White Sauce, 120
Bread Pudding, 217
Bread Stuffing, 196
Broccoli-Cauliflower-Celery, 107
Broken Glass Salad, 160
Brown Gravy, 202
Brussels Sprouts, 108

Cabbage au Gratin, 108
Cabbage Holland Style, 109
Cabbage Rolls, 33

Calico Beans, 101
Canadian Bacon-Squash Casserole, 128
Candied Sweet Potatoes, 130
Carrot and Raisin Salad, 161
Carrot Loaf, 112
Carrots Supreme, 112
Cauliflower with Cheese, 113
Celery, Creole Style, 113
Celery Seed Dressing, 211
Celery and Tomatoes, 113
Cheddar-Crab Casserole, 92
Cheddar Steak, 34
Cheese and Tuna Casserole, 87
Cheese Beef Loaf, 35
Cheese Sauce, 202
Cheese Soufflé, 191
Cheese with Seafood or Vegetable Soufflé, 191
Cherry-Chocolate Treat, 218
Cherry Chicken Mold, 148
Cherry Salad, 161
Chestnut Stuffing, 196
Chicken a la Kiev, 68
Chicken a la King, 69
Chicken-Asparagus Casserole, 63
Chicken Basque, 64
Chicken Cacciatore, 64
Chicken Casserole, 65
Chicken Croquettes, 66
Chicken Diet Plate, 149
Chicken-Green Bean Casserole, 67
Chicken Livers Stroganoff, 69
Chicken Marengo, 70
Chicken with Noodles, 71
Chicken Patties, 72
Chicken and Potato Chowder, 186
Chicken Pot Pie, 72
Chicken Rococo, 73
Chicken Spaghetti, 75
Chicken Wings, 181
Chinese Cabbage, 111
Chinese Eggplant, 116
Chinese Vegetables, 114

Chive and Wild Rice Stuffing for Game, 197
Chocolate Eclairs, 218
Chop Suey, 59
Chow Mein, 59
Clam Chowder, 186
Club Salad, 166
Cocktail Sauce, 203
Codfish Cakes, 81
Cole Slaw, 162
Cole Slaw Dressing, 211
Corn Bread, 199
Corn and Tomato Pudding, 115
Corned Beef Salad, 147
Cornish Hens and Wild Rice, 77
Crab Canapés, 181
Crab Pilaf, 141
Cranberry Holiday Salad, 167
Cranberry Sauce Salad, 168
Cream of Chicken and Noodles, 71
Creamed Codfish, 81
Creamed Cucumbers, 115
Creamed Radishes, 127
Creamed Smoked Salmon, 85
Creamed Vegetable Casserole, 118
Creole Sauce, 203
Creole Sweet Potatoes, 131
Crimson Glaze, 204
Crystal Salad, 168
Cucumber Relish, 169
Cucumbers and Onion Relish, 169
Cucumbers in Sour Cream Dressing, 169
Curried South African Rock Lobster Tails, 96
Curried Tuna, 87
Custard Sauce, 204

Deviled Eggs, 182
Deviled Egg Salad, 149
Dill Sauce, 204
Dipping Sauce, 204
Drambuie Chicken, 66

Title Index

Dried Beef Casserole, 23
Dumplings, 200
Dutch Beets, 106
Dutch-Style Red Cabbage, 109

Easy Baked Beans, 102
Easy Chicken and Rice Casserole, 66
Easy Chili Con Carne with Beans, 35
Easy Goulash, 37
Easy Lasagne, 39
Easy Potato Soup, 188
Eggplant Casserole, 115
Eggplant Creole, 116
Eggplant Parmesan, 117
Eggplant Stroganoff, 118
Emerald Relish, 170
Everlasting Salad, 165

Fettuccini with Chives, 143
Fiesta Chicken Bake, 67
Fish 'n' Chips Casserole, 88
Fisherman's Chowder, 187
Five-Cup Fruit Fancy, 170
Foamy Sauce, 205
Fondue with Rock Lobster, 96
Four-Bean Salad, 159
French-Fried Onion Rings, 121
French-Fried Oysters, 98
French Green Beans, 103
Fresh Cranberry Salad, 167
Fresh Fruit Salad, 171
Fresh Salmon Baked or Grilled, 82
Fresh Vegetable Chowder, 189
Fried Chicken Southern Style, 68
Fried Chicken Vichyssoise, 76
Fried Cornmeal Mush, 199
Fried Eggplant, 117
Fried Fish, 82
Fried Green Tomatoes, 133
Fried Heart, 23
Fried Mushrooms, 119

Fried Onions, 120
Fried Rice, 139
Fruit Salad Dressing, 212

Garlic Bread, 198
Gen's Famous Egg Salad, 150
Glazed Carrots, 111
Glazed Ham, 49
Glazed Onions, 121
Glazed Squash, 129
Golden-Egg Rich Potato Salad, 175
Green Bean and Dried Beef Luncheon Dish, 26
Green Bean Fritters, 103
Green Beans Italiano, 103
Green Beans Supreme, 104
Green Beans and Water Chestnuts, 105
Ground Beef and Cabbage Casserole, 34
Ground Beef and Dumplings, 37

Ham Loaf, 50
Ham-Macaroni Casserole, 50
Ham with Noodles and Mushrooms, 50
Ham Salad, 150
Ham Sandwich Spread Salad, 150
Hamburger Casserole for Twelve, 38
Hamburger Spaghetti, 38
Hard Sauce, 205
Harvard Beets, 106
Hash, 24
Hawaiian Marinade, 205
Heavenly Hash, 219
Herbed Sour Cream Dressing, 213
Hollandaise Sauce, 206
Holland-Style Apple Salad, 155
Horseradish Sauce, 206
Hot Deviled Potatoes, 124
Hot Sauerkraut, 128
Hush Puppies, 200

Title Index

Idaho Pizza, 125
Indian Pudding, 220
Irish Coffee, 221
Irish Stew, 57
Italian-Style Zucchini, 136

Jack's Chinese Special, 39
Jack Spratt's Platter, 76
Jellied Salmon Salad, 151

Kidney Bean Salad, 158
Knockwurst with Sauerkraut and Sweet Potatoes, 57

Lamb Curry, 57
Layered Salad, 171
Lebanese Cabbage Rolls, 33
Lemon-Garlic Butter, 206
Lettuce Salad, 172
Lime Salad, 176
Liver Loaf, 58
Lobster Thermidor, 97

Macaroni and Cheese, 143
Macaroni Creole, 144
Macaroni Goulash, 41
Macaroni and Ham Cole Slaw, 164
Mashed Potatoes, 125
Mashed Turnips, 134
Meatballs, 39
Meat Loaf I, 40
Meat Loaf II, 41
Meat Loaf Patties, 41
Mincemeat Lemon Sauce, 207
Mock Chicken Legs, 51
Moist Bread Stuffing, 196
Molded Cole Slaw, 163
Mom's Cabbage Salad, 162
Mustard Beans, 159
Mustard Sauce, 207

New England Boiled Dinner, 24

Okra, Rice, and Tomatoes, 119
Old-Fashioned Cooked Salad Dressing, 212
Onion Delight, 120
Onion-Potatoes, 122
Orange-Butter Sauce, 207
Orange Waldorf Salad, 178
Oriental Chicken, 70
Oriental Stew, 26
Oven-Fried Parmesan Chicken, 71
Oyster Cocktail, 182
Oyster Stew, 187
Oyster Stuffing, 197

Parsley-Butter for Seafood or Potatoes, 208
Parsley Rice, 140
Parsleyed New Potatoes, 126
Parsnip Fritters, 122
Party Cranberry Salad, 168
Party Mold, 148
Pear Cranberry Salad, 173
Pear Salad, 172
Pennsylvania Dutch-Style Green Beans, 104
Pepper Hamburger Steak, 42
Pepper Steak, 26
Perfection Relish Salad, 173
Perfection Salad, 173
Pickled Beets, 160
Pickled Bologna, 147
Pickled Eggs, 160
Pink or Green or Orange Salad, 174
Pigs in a Blanket, 27
Piquant Sauce, 208
Plain Soufflé, 192
Plantation Supper, 42
Poppy Seed Dressing, 212
Porcupine Meatballs, 40
Pork Chops and Rice, 53
Pork Chops and Sweet Potatoes, 53

Title Index

Pork Hocks or Ham Hocks, 55
Pork Steak, 55
Pot Roast, 27
Potato Puff, 126
Potato Salad Loaf, 175
Potato Soufflé, 192

Quick Corned Beef and Cabbage, 22
Quick Jelly Roll Dough, 220
Quick-Molded Crab Salad, 149
Quick Tamale Pie, 47

Rabbit Loaf, 58
Ranch-Style Baked Beans, 42
Raspberry Marshmallow Fruit Mold, 176
Raspberry Salad, 175
Raw Cauliflower, 161
Red Cabbage with Apples, 109
Red Cabbage Cole Slaw, 164
Red Cardinal Cole Slaw, 164
Red and Green Cole Slaw, 165
Rice au Gratin, 139
Rice O'Brien, 140
Rigatoni for Twenty, 43
Roast Chicken, 73
Roquefort or Blue Cheese Sauce, 208

Saffron Rice Ring, 140
Salad Con Carne, 36
Salisbury Steak, 43
Salmonburgers, 83
Salmon Dinner Roll, 83
Salmon Loaf, 84
Salmon Parmesan, 84
Salmon Patties, 85
Salmon Puff, 85
Salmon Salad, 152
Salmon Soufflé, 193
Sauerkraut Salad, 177
Sausage and Succotash, 59
Sautéed Parsnips, 122

Scalloped Cabbage with Cheese, 110
Scalloped Corn, 114
Scalloped Eggplant, 117
Scalloped Oysters, 98
Scalloped Oysters and Corn, 98
Scalloped Parsnips, 123
Scalloped Potatoes, 126
Scalloped Potatoes and Ham, 127
Scrapple, 60
Sesame Chicken, 74
Seven-Layer Vegetable Casserole, 135
Shepherd's Pie, 28
Shoofly Pie, 221
Shrimp Canapés, 183
Shrimp Cantonese, 99
Shrimp Cocktail, 183
Shrimp Creole, 100
Simmered Red Cabbage, 110
Snowtop Mandarin Mold, 177
Sour Cream Chive for Baked Potato, 208
South African Gourmet Salad, 151
South African Rock Lobster Newburg, 97
Southern Pudding, 142
Spaghetti Meat Sauce, 44
Spam Polynesian, 60
Spanish Chicken and Rice, 75
Spanish Lima Beans, 105
Spanish Rice, 44
Spanish Sauce, 209
Spanish Steak, 29
Spicy Applesauce Mold, 156
Spicy Peach Salad, 172
Split Pea Soup, 188
Squash with Bacon, 129
Squash Mandarin, 130
Steamed Clams, 91
Stewed Cabbage, 110
Stewed Tomatoes, 134
Stroganoff Pie, 45
Stuffed Green Peppers, 45, 123

Stuffed Mushrooms, 182
Stuffed Pork Chops, 54
Stuffed Zucchini, 137
Succotash, 133
Sunshine Rice, 142
Super Supper, 46
Swedish Cabbage, 166
Sweet 'n' Sour Pork Oriental, 56
Sweet Potato Casserole, 131
Sweet Potato Pie, 132
Sweet Potato Puff, 132
Sweet-Sour Cabbage, 111
Sweet-Sour Meatballs with Red Cabbage, 46
Sweet-Sour Sauce, 209
Swiss Steak, 29

Tamale Pie for a Dozen, 47
Tamale Pie with Noodles, 48
Tartar Sauce, 209
Tenderloin of Beef Stroganoff with Wild Rice, 40
Tenderloin Tips in Burgundy, 30
Thousand Island Dressing, 213
Three-Bean Salad, 159
Tomato Steak, 31
Tuna Barbecue, 86
Tuna Broccoli, 86
Tuna Delight, 88
Tuna Florentine, 89
Tuna Italiano, 89
Tuna Jambalaya, 89
Tuna Loaf, 152
Tuna Mousse, 153

Tuna-Noodles with Cheddar Cheese, 90
Tuna Pilaf, 141
Tuna Romanoff, 90
Tuna Salad, 152
Tuna Sandwich Spread Salad, 152
Tuna Soufflé with Bacon, 193
Tuna Stroganoff, 90
Tuna Tetrazzini, 91
Tuna Waldorf Salad, 153
Turkey Hawaiian, 78
Turkey Tetrazzini, 79
Turnip Soufflé, 194
Twice-Baked Potatoes, 124

Veal Parmesan, 61
Vegetable Chowder, 189
Velouté Sauce, 210
Venison with Onion, 61

Waldorf Salad, 178
Welsh Rarebit, 210
White Sauce, 210
Wild Rice Casserole, 143
Wine Pot Roast, 28
World War II Homemade Mayonnaise, 213

Yams and Pineapple, 133
Yorkshire Pudding, 198

Zucchini Casserole, 135
Zucchini Creole, 136
Zucchini-Eggplant Casserole, 136
Zucchini Parmesan, 137